INDEPENDENCE TOWNSHIP LIBRARY

3 4633 00102 3090

WITHDRAWN

D0108706

Donated in Memory of
Ellen H. Curry-Pollock

John & Elaine Sharrock

A NEW OWNER'S
GUIDE TO
LHASA APSOS

JG-148

Overleaf: A Lhasa Apso adult and puppy photographed by Isabelle Francais.

Opposite page: An adult Lhasa Apso.

The Publisher wishes to acknowledge the following owners of the dogs in this book: Jan and Larry Bruton, Stephen G. C. Campbell, Leslie Ann Engen, Toni Rae Fiorello, Jo Ann Germano, Linda Jarrett, Phyllis Marcy, Marianne Nixon, Sherry Owens, Nancy Plunkett, Kathie Ruffner, Leslie and Jesse Warren, Bobbie Wood.

Photographers: Jan and Larry Bruton, Callea Photo, Tara Darling, Leslie Ann Engen, Isabelle Francais, Bruce and Jeane Harkins, Nancy Plunkett, Vince Serbin, Robert Smith.

The author acknowledges the contribution of Judy Iby for the following chapters in this book: Sport of Purebred Dogs, Health Care, Identification and Finding the Lost Dog, Traveling with Your Dog, and Behavior and Canine Communication.

The portrayal of canine pet products in this book is for general instructive value only; the appearance of such products does not necessarily constitute an endorsement by the authors, the publisher, or the owners of the dogs portrayed in this book.

3 4633 00102 3090

(t.f.h.)

© by T.F.H. Publications, Inc.

Distributed in the UNITED STATES to the Pet Trade by T.F.H. Publications, Inc., One T.F.H. Plaza, Neptune City, NJ 07753; on the Internet at www.tfh.com; in CANADA Rolf C. Hagen Inc., 3225 Sartelon St. Laurent-Montreal Quebec H4R 1E8; Pet Trade by H & L Pet Supplies Inc., 27 Kingston Crescent, Kitchener, Ontario N2B 2T6; in ENGLAND by T.F.H. Publications, PO Box 15, Waterlooville PO7 6BQ; in AUSTRALIA AND THE SOUTH PACIFIC by T.F.H. (Australia), Pty. Ltd., Box 149, Brookvale 2100 N.S.W., Australia; in NEW ZEALAND by Brooklands Aquarium Ltd. 5 McGiven Drive, New Plymouth, RD1 New Zealand; in SOUTH AFRICA, Rolf C. Hagen S.A. (PTY.) LTD. P.O. Box 201199, Durban North 4016, South Africa; in Japan by T.F.H. Publications, Japan—Jiro Tsuda, 10-12-3 Ohjidai, Sakura, Chiba 285, Japan. Published by T.F.H. Publications, Inc.

MANUFACTURED IN THE
UNITED STATES OF AMERICA
BY T.F.H. PUBLICATIONS, INC.

A New Owner's
Guide to
LHASA APSOS

Nancy Plunkett

Contents

1998 Edition

The Lhasa was highly prized as a guardian in his native Tibet.

A Lhasa puppy will always want to be in on the action!

The Lhasa Apso's long coat gives
him his distinctive appearance.

It's hard to resist the
adorable Lhasa puppy.

Your Lhasa Apso will look to you for the
guidance and discipline he needs.

HISTORY and Origin of the Lhasa Apso

Mankind's love of dogs extends back into the earliest mists of time when wolf and human first met and began a mutual journey toward civilization and domestication. That *Canis lupus*, the wolf, assisted mankind along this path is a historical fact. And it is man himself that can be credited for the wolf's journey from creature of the forest to *Canis familiaris*, the domesticated dog.

The Lhasa Apso was highly prized in his native Tibet because it was believed that he could protect his owners from evil spirits.

Companion and purely ornamental toy breeds are known to have existed even before dynastic times in Egypt. Pictures of very small, lightly colored dogs with silken coats appear on urns and vases excavated from the ruins of ancient Greece. These are thought to be descendants of a northern, more wolf-like dog developed as early as Neolithic times resembling today's spitz-type breeds.

Extensive research has been done by canine historians Richard and Alice Fiennes into the development of the individual canine breeds in their excellent book, *The Natural History of Dogs*. The Fienneses are convinced that small companion-type dogs also existed throughout the Roman Empire and were traded to Tibet. The Tibetans at that time enjoyed trade with China and there can be little doubt that the dogs that had made their way from Egypt to Rome and thence to Tibet also had influence in the development of China's *ha pa* dogs. The term *ha pa*, meaning "under the table dogs," has particular significance in that it relates to the small dogs that fit under the tables used in China at that time, which were about eight inches high. It is highly likely that these *ha pa* dogs made their way back along the caravan routes to Tibet as well.

Tibetan peasants kept large dogs that lived outdoors, guarding flocks, and protected their owners from intruders. In the unlikely event that unwanted guests managed to make their way past these ferocious mastiff-type dogs, the peasants offered themselves double protection by keeping small alarm

dogs indoors. The likelihood of an intruder slipping by the outdoor guards was remote, so there seems ample proof that the little indoor dogs served to guard their people against the evil spirits who, with their clever ways, could elude the larger dogs.

REINCARNATED BEINGS

The common people were not likely to worry about pure blood in their dogs, and though most of the monasteries had a large population of dogs, they did not practice any sort of breeding program either. The most we can assume is that the monks kept their favorite dogs in close proximity, and those animals were allowed to breed freely. Dogs were frequently given away by the monks as political gifts of friendship, so it was necessary to maintain their canine population in order to supply that demand. The monks believed, as they still do now, that the dogs were, in fact, reincarnated beings on just one part of their spiritual journey toward Nirvana.

Realistically, the development of the Lhasa Apso owes more to Tibet as a country than it does to the Tibetan people. Although the Tibetans were of a theological society believing in a peaceful coexistence with their animals, it was the severe environment of Tibet that dictated the specific physical and mental characteristics of the little dogs that developed. Their small, sturdy, longer-than-tall bodies enabled them to conserve heat while still allowing them the agility to negotiate the mountainous terrain. The dogs' straight, heavy, and hard coat texture protected them from the elements without the coat itself becoming a burdensome or life-threatening liability.

Tibet's isolation from the rest of the world instilled a healthy mistrust of strangers in the dogs and gave them an uncanny ability to instantly distinguish friend from foe. The harsh environment forced the Lhasa Apso to develop a somewhat tough and independent character. There was no coddling in this primitive country, and self-sufficiency was necessary for survival. The dogs had to be healthy, they had to be tough, and they had to be smart in order to live and reproduce.

The Lhasa Apso was never sold, only given as a gift of friendship. Those remaining at home were annually shorn along with the other livestock, and their hair was spun and woven into warm woolen garments. The Lhasa Apso's "wool" is extremely warm and water repellent, resembling the wool taken from Icelandic sheep. It is said that stories were handed down along with each garment, telling of the Lhasa from whose coat it had been made.

THE LHASA JOURNEYS WESTWARD

In 1901, the first Lhasa Apsos made their way to England. Their success and popularity in that country was immediate. The breed, under the name "Lhasa Terrier," was granted separate classification by The Kennel Club in England. By 1908, the breed had grown and had been awarded championship status. World War I abruptly changed the picture, however. The core stock was so dramatically devastated that almost nothing remained and the Kennel Club was forced to withdraw the Lhasa's eligibility to achieve championship status.

Originally, the beautiful Lhasa was never sold but given to people as a token of luck or gratitude.

It was not until 1928 that the breed was able to regain a

foothold in England through imports. Unfortunately, some of the dogs exported from China to the United Kingdom were to prove as much a problem as they were a remedy to the depleted breeding stock. Some were not, in fact, Lhasa Apsos, but actually Shih Tzu.

THE LHASA IN AMERICA

The prestigious Hamilton Farms of Mr. & Mrs. C. Suydam Cutting imported the first Lhasa Apsos to the US in the early 1930s. Hamilton Farms was a 5,000-acre estate in Gladstone, New Jersey, now the home of the US Equestrian team. The kennels were managed by the team of James Anderson and Fred Huyler, who not only showed the dogs for the Cuttings but were also responsible for developing a highly successful breeding program.

Because of early crosses with the Shih Tzu, shown here, a vast majority of Lhasa Apsos bred in the US can trace their pedigrees back to this breed.

In 1935, the American Kennel Club gave the breed official recognition and the American breed standard was approved. The breed was known as the "Lhasa Terrier" in the US, as it was in England, and was shown under that name until 1944, when the name was changed to Lhasa Apso. Although the terrier suffix was removed from the Lhasa's name, it was still shown in the AKC Terrier Group until 1959, when it was moved to the Non-Sporting Group.

THE SHIH TZU SCANDAL

Between the years 1937 and 1950, seven dogs were imported from England that were registered as Lhasa Apsos,

The Lhasa Apso's keen intelligence and steadfast loyalty make him an excellent companion. but were of the blood of the Shih Tzus that had entered England from China. Before the AKC realized these dogs were actually a different breed, they had already been used extensively in many Lhasa Apso breeding programs in the US. Only Hamilton Farms did not incorporate the Shih Tzus into their breeding program. The Hamilton dogs were bred and shown extensively until after the death of Mrs. Cutting in 1961, when her husband sold most of the dogs to Mrs. Dorothy Cohen, whose Karma kennels were located in Las Vegas, Nevada.

The "Straight Hamilton" bloodline still exists today, though it is in the minority. The vast majority of US Lhasa Apsos can trace a large portion of their pedigrees to those early Shih Tzu crosses.

The Lhasa Apso parent club was founded in 1959. BIS Ch. SanJo Hussel Bussel, ROM, helps celebrate the American Lhasa Apso Club's 25th anniversary.

THE PARENT CLUB IS FOUNDED

Undaunted by what could easily be called the "Shih Tzu Scandal," and true to its resolute heritage, the Lhasa not only survived but also flourished in America. In February of 1959, 14 dedicated fanciers founded the American Lhasa Apso Club (ALAC), naming Mr. C. Suydam Cutting as Honorary President and Fred Huyler, who had managed Mr. Cutting's Hamilton Farms kennel, as the group's first president and treasurer. There were 250 Lhasa Apsos registered with the AKC in the following year.

The ALAC held its first Specialty show in conjunction with the Trenton Kennel Club in 1966, with all-breed judge Mr. James Trullinger presiding. Mr. Trullinger chose Ch. Kham of Norbulingka, owned by Phyllis Marcy, as Best of Breed.

The year 1957 was important for the Lhasa Apso, for on October 26, the female Ch. Hamilton Torma made history. She became the first of her breed to win an all-breed Best In Show in the US. Torma was not only a winner of consequence; she was a producer of outstanding merit for her owner, Mrs. Marie Stillman's American Kennels in Beverly Hills, California.

Since that memorable first Best In Show, Lhasas have become one of the Non-Sporting Group's most formidable contenders for top laurels. Outstanding winners and significant kennels can be found throughout the country. The breed has also become well known as a delightful companion. At the close of the AKC's 1996 registration year, the Lhasa Apso ranked No. 33 among the 143 breeds recognized by that organization. There were 11,903 Lhasas registered in that year alone.

A hardy breed, the Lhasa Apso has evolved over many centuries, surviving harsh climates and difficult terrain.

A SAD POSTSCRIPT

Although the Lhasa Apso has flourished in the United States and many other parts of the world, neither the breed nor its people have enjoyed this happy state in their homeland. In 1959, communist China waged a full-scale invasion of Tibet. In the ensuing years, the Chinese army killed well over a million Tibetans and destroyed over 6,000 of their monasteries in an attempt to eradicate the Tibetan culture. Tibetan dogs were killed along with the people as the Chinese army advanced into Tibet, because the Communist Party considered dogs "a decadent bourgeois luxury."

Many Tibetans, including the Dalai Lama, were able to flee to neighboring countries such as India, Bhutan, and Nepal, where they wait for the day they can return to their homeland. The Lhasa Apso can be seen in many of these refugee communities today, living in exile along with the Tibetan people.

CHARACTERISTICS of the Lhasa Apso

Before anyone tries to decide whether the Lhasa Apso is the correct breed for him or her, a larger, more important question must be asked. That question is, "Should I own any dog at all?" Dog ownership is a serious and time-consuming responsibility that should not be entered into lightly. Failure to understand this can make what should be a rewarding relationship one of sheer drudgery. It is also one of the primary reasons that thousands upon thousands of unwanted dogs end their lives in humane societies and animal shelters throughout America.

Inquisitive and curious, the Lhasa will always want to be a part of the action.

If the prospective dog owner lives alone and conditions are conducive to dog ownership, all he or she needs do is be sure that there is a strong desire to make the necessary commitment that dog ownership entails. In the case of family households, the situation is a much more complicated one. It is vital that the person who will actually be responsible for the dog's care really wants a dog.

In many households, mothers are most often given the additional responsibility of caring for the family pets. Children are away at school all day. Father is at work. Often it is the mother—even when she, too, works outside of the home—who is saddled with the additional chores of housebreaking, feeding, and trips to the veterinary hospital. What was supposed to be a family project somehow manages to become solely her responsibility.

Nearly all children love puppies and dogs and will promise anything to get one. But childhood

Puppies are hard to resist, but make sure you carefully consider the responsibilities of dog ownership.

enthusiasm can wane very quickly and it becomes up to the adults in the family to ensure the dog receives proper care. Children should be taught responsibility, but to expect a living, breathing, and needy animal to teach a child this lesson is to be incredibly indifferent to the needs of the animal.

There are also many households in which the entire family is gone from early morning until late in the day. The question that must be asked then is, "Who will provide food for the dog and access to the outdoors if the dog is expected not to relieve himself in the house?" This is something that can probably be worked out with an adult dog, but it is totally unfair for anyone to expect a young puppy to be left alone the entire day without an accident.

Should an individual or family find that they are capable of providing the proper home for a dog or young puppy, suitability of breed must also be considered. Here it might be worthwhile to look at the difference between owning a purebred dog and one of mixed ancestry.

A purebred Lhasa Apso will most likely grow up to look and act like his parents.

The Case for the Purebred Dog

A mongrel can give you as much love and devotion as a purebred dog. However, the manner in which the dog does this and how his personality, energy level, and the amount of care he requires suits an individual's lifestyle are major considerations. In a purebred dog, most of these considerations are predictable to a marked degree, even if the dog is purchased as a very young puppy. A puppy of uncertain parentage will not give you this insurance.

All puppies are cute and manageable, but someone who lives in a two-room apartment will find life difficult with a dog that grows to the size of a Great Dane. Nor is the mountain climber or marathon runner going to be happy with an extremely short-nosed breed that has difficulty catching his breath while simply walking across the street on a hot summer day.

An owner who expects his or her dog to sit quietly by their side while his master watches television or reads is not going to be particularly happy with a high-strung, off-the-wall dog whose rest requirements are only 30

Make sure the breed of dog you are considering will fit into your home, family, and lifestyle.

seconds out of every ten hours! The outdoorsman is not going to be particularly happy with a breed whose coat attracts every burr, leaf, and insect in all of nature.

Knowing what kind of dog best suits your lifestyle is not just a consideration, it is paramount to the foundation of your lifelong relationship with the dog. If the dog you are considering does not fit your lifestyle, the relationship simply will not last.

Life With A Lhasa Apso

All of the foregoing points apply when deciding if you should own a Lhasa Apso. Further, as appealing as a pudgy and fluffy Lhasa Apso puppy might be, remember that he is a long-coated dog and that coat needs care, even when it is kept conveniently short. Regular brushing and bathing is necessary. When the Lhasa Apso is outdoors, it is no less a dog than any other. He enjoys playing in the mud, burying himself in the sandbox, or rolling in the brambles as much as any other breed would. His coat should be dealt with immediately.

The Lhasa Apso is a breed that will only stay healthy and looking like a Lhasa Apso as long as you are willing to invest the time in keeping him that way. If you do not feel you have the time to do this yourself, it will be necessary to have a professional groomer do this for you. If you appreciate the long-coated look of the breed, realize that it will take more than a little effort on your part to keep it looking that way.

The breed is a hardy one and if purchased from a responsible breeder is seldom prone to chronic illnesses. It is a naturally playful and inquisitive

In terms of grooming, the Lhasa is a high-maintenance dog. The time you wish to spend on grooming should be a consideration before choosing a breed.

The rugged remote environment of Tibet has contributed to shaping the Lhasa's sturdy conformation and independent character.

breed. The Lhasa Apso is never without having something to do, yet just as content to sit by your side when you read or listen to music.

MALE OR FEMALE?

There is one important point to consider in determining your choice between male and female. While both must be trained not to relieve themselves just anywhere in the home, males that have not been neutered have a natural instinct to lift their leg and urinate to "mark" their home territory.

It seems confusing to many dog owners, but a male's marking of his home turf has absolutely nothing to do with whether or not he is housebroken. The two responses come from entirely different needs and must be dealt with in that manner. Some dogs are more difficult to train not to mark within the confines of the household than others are. Males that are used for breeding are even more prone to this response and even harder to break of doing so.

On the other hand, a male Lhasa generally seems to enjoy obedience work more than the female, though both have been trained with equal success.

Females have their semiannual "heat" cycles once they have reached sexual maturity. In the case of the female Lhasa Apso, this can occur for the first time at about nine or ten months of age. These cycles are accompanied by a vaginal discharge that creates the need to confine the female for about three weeks so that she does not soil her surroundings. It must be understood the female has no control over this bloody discharge, so it has nothing to do with training.

This is one time a female should not be outdoors by herself for even a brief moment or two. The need for confinement and to keep a careful watch over the female in heat is especially important to prevent her from becoming pregnant by some neighborhood Lothario. Equally dangerous to her well-being is the male that is much larger than your Lhasa Apso female. The dog may be too large to actually breed with her, but he could seriously injure or even kill her in his attempts to do so.

By spaying the female and neutering the male, these sexually related problems could be eliminated. Unless a Lhasa Apso has been purchased expressly for breeding or showing from a breeder capable of making this judgment, it is highly recommended that your dog be sexually altered.

There are other benefits of spaying and neutering. Bitches who have not been spayed are at high risk for uterine infections, especially as they get older. This is a serious and potentially fatal illness. Early spaying almost completely eliminates the risk of mammary tumors, which are very common and often malignant in older intact bitches. Intact males can suffer from testicular cancer and prostate problems.

Breeding and raising puppies should be left in the hands of people who have the facilities to keep each puppy they

Breeding should only be done by someone who has the knowledge, time, and facilities to care for the mother and all the puppies involved.

Reputable breeders will screen all prospective Lhasas to ensure against genetic diseases and produce the best puppies possible.

breed until the correct home is found for them. This can often take many months after a litter is born. Most single dog owners are not equipped to do this. Naturally, a responsible Lhasa Apso owner would never allow his or her pet to roam the streets and end his life in an animal shelter. Unfortunately, being forced to place a puppy before you are able to thoroughly check out the prospective buyer may, in fact, create this exact situation.

Many times parents ask to buy a female just as a pet, but with full intentions of breeding so that their children can witness the birth process. There are countless books and videos now available that portray this wonderful event and do not add to the worldwide pet overpopulation we now face. Altering one's companion dogs not only precludes the possibility of adding to this problem, it eliminates bothersome household problems and precautions.

It should be understood, however, that spaying and neutering are not reversible procedures. Spayed females and neutered males are not allowed to be shown in American Kennel Club shows, nor will altered animals ever be able to be used for breeding.

THE LHASA APSO PERSONALITY

The character of the Lhasa Apso is both complex and individualistic. Therefore, it is vitally important to know as much as possible about the breed before deciding to bring one into your home. Centuries of natural selection in such a unique environment as Tibet have created a dog with an interesting combination of character traits. The breed is intensely devoted to its people yet maintains its independence in ways that are a constant challenge.

Over 60 years of breeding in the United States has mellowed temperaments somewhat, but this still is not a breed for the soft-willed or faint of heart. The Lhasa Apso breed standard of 1935 stated, "Gay and assertive, but chary of strangers." This is an excellent description of their character.

The Lhasa Apso is happy and confident as a rule, and is a wonderfully affectionate companion. They live to be near you, thrive on your attention, and have empathic abilities that are a never-ending source of comfort, enjoyment, and downright amazement. The Lhasa Apso's semi-domestic background in Tibet has endowed the breed with intelligence beyond the norm. Their creative problem-solving abilities are always entertaining to observe, though one must always be on one's toes in order to stay ahead of them.

Personalities differ greatly from individual to individual, but there are some common threads. Without exception, they have a deep and abiding need for human companionship. They are extremely possessive of their things (and this conceivably includes you, toys, food, house, yard, car, or crate). Strangers and things out of the ordinary are suspect until proven harmless and above all, the Lhasa Apso always has his own interests foremost in mind no matter *what* he is doing. Each of these traits is the foundation, or motivation, for most everything the Lhasa Apso does in life, both good and bad.

No description of the Lhasa Apso character would be complete without mention of their tendency to be assertive. While it can be part of their charm, the Lhasa Apso's assertiveness can also be a source of trouble for many pet owners. Centuries of learning to be self-reliant in Tibet has given this breed a mind of its own and they do not always submit easily to having someone tell them what they can and cannot do. Call it what you will—independent, stubborn, willful, or headstrong—it translates into an animal that requires an equal amount of determination from its owners. The typical Lhasa Apso absolutely delights in challenging authority and never completely gives up hope of gaining ground in the ongoing battle of wills, often testing the boundaries of permitted behavior just to see if he can get away with it. Owners must be prepared to deal with this facet of the Lhasa Apso character with equal parts of understanding, discipline, and patience. It is also somewhat helpful to have a healthy sense of humor.

The Lhasa's fearless nature and confidence allow him to adapt to any situation. Ch. Chenrezi Rain Bo's End, owned by Larry Bruton, plows ahead in the snow.

The Lhasa Apso also tends to be somewhat wary or suspicious of strangers. It is difficult for many to believe that these invitingly adorable little bundles of fur are so

Although wary of strangers at first, the Lhasa Apso will devote himself to the people he loves.

discriminating with their affection, but in this case, appearances are truly deceiving. The typical Lhasa Apso will stand back from strangers on first acquaintance and will prefer not to be touched by them until he is certain that it is "safe." Often it is just a moment or two until he is comfortable with newcomers, then he will make it a point to investigate them as thoroughly as possible before settling down somewhere close by to watch.

Trying to force the Lhasa Apso to make friends before he is ready will usually have just the opposite effect than the one desired, making him more suspicious than ever. The easiest way to establish a friendship with a Lhasa Apso is for the stranger to totally ignore the dog's presence until he has decided the stranger is no longer a threat. Even then, the person's gestures should be kept polite and not overly familiar, and eye contact should be kept to a minimum. Premature or aggressive actions by a stranger will delay acceptance accordingly. Once the friendship is truly solid, the Lhasa will relax and share unlimited affection. Anyone with hostile or deceitful intent will never gain the trust of the keenly astute Lhasa Apso.

A particularly endearing trait of the breed is an incredible sensitivity to emotion. They seem to be able to read a person's heart without fail and will react to each emotion in their own personal way. Happiness, grief, anger—

The Lhasa loves to be in the company of people and can be very protective of those he considers part of his family.

whatever the emotion is, your Lhasa will know and will communicate to you his return feelings. For instance, we once had our one-year-old female, Purity, at our veterinarian for her rabies booster. There was a woman sitting

near us with a very old dog wrapped in a blanket. The dog was obviously failing rapidly and the distressed woman was weeping. Purity watched her for a few minutes and then walked over to the woman, sat down in front of her and started whining quietly with concern. Purity would glance over at me to make sure I saw, almost as though she was hoping I could do something for the poor woman. It brought *me* to tears!

TYPICAL BEHAVIOR PATTERNS

The Lhasa Apso tends to be a vocal breed. They will sound the alarm whenever they see, hear, or smell something out of the ordinary. In addition to barking in defense, the Lhasa Apso's somewhat demanding nature may also find voice at times of anticipation, impatience, and excitement. The Lhasa *will* bark to bring attention to those things he considers important. This is a quality inherent to the breed and must be taken into account by pet owners.

Jealousy and possessiveness can be a common source of problems in multidog households. This is often a point of debate between puppy and owner and must be dealt with at the onset. The Lhasa Apso can be dog aggressive and he is not intimidated by the size of even the largest dog. Obedience training can help here.

The Lhasa Apso has quite a wicked sense of humor that is often at human expense. The breed is extremely creative when it comes to thinking up "games" to play. (You can almost see them laughing at you!)

The Lhasa has an unquenchable need to be with you—not just nearby, but *with* you, and is apt to be inadvertently locked in closets, spare rooms, bathrooms, and garages. At times they are so close behind you, you might think they are among the missing.

"Smiling" is something quite common among Lhasas. Their habit of grinning when feeling some

There is nothing a Lhasa likes better than making mischief! The breed's sense of humor and creativity never ceases to amaze his owners.

How can you resist a Lhasa smile? The Lhasa Apso is well known for his sensitivity to his loved one's feelings. strong emotion is unique and charming. To those unfamiliar with a dog smile, it can look threatening but it is just another way the breed has of expressing itself.

The Lhasa Apso likes to be up high—surveying his vast domain, no doubt. They are also good climbers, very cat-like, and are not above trying to reach the tabletops. They also love secret little dens where they can be secluded and protected from above and all sides.

Lhasas are inclined to be thieves, pack rats, scavengers, and even sneaks. If something of yours is missing, check your Lhasa's favorite den or hiding place.

Predatory behavior in many Lhasa Apsos is no doubt the result of their background in Tibet. Not only will they catch and eat many large insects, if given the chance they will also quickly dispatch and consume small rodents and birds. No amount of discouragement seems to curb this instinct.

STANDARD for the Lhasa Apso

The AKC standard of the Lhasa Apso is written in simple straightforward language that can be read and understood by even the beginning fancier. However, its implications take many years to fully understand. This can only be accomplished through observing many show-quality Lhasa Apsos over the years and reading as much about the breed as possible.

A good many books have been written about the breed and it is well worth the Lhasa Apso owner's time and effort to digest their contents if he or she is interested in showing or breeding.

Some breeds change drastically from puppyhood to adulthood. It would be extremely difficult for the untrained eye to determine the actual breed of some purebred dogs in puppyhood. This is not quite so with the Lhasa Apso outside of the length of the mature dog's coat. In fact, at eight weeks of age, the actual conformation of a Lhasa Apso puppy will reflect in miniature what he will look like, in many respects, at maturity.

It must be remembered that a breed standard describes the "perfect" Lhasa Apso, but no dog is perfect and no Lhasa Apso, not even the greatest dog show winner, will possess every quality asked for in its perfect form. How closely an individual dog adheres to the standard of the breed determines his show potential.

The Lhasa Apso's coat should be heavy, straight, and hard, possessing length and density.

OFFICAL STANDARD FOR THE LHASA APSO

Character—Gay and assertive, but chary of strangers.

Size—Variable, but about 10 inches or 11 inches at shoulder for dogs, bitches slightly smaller.

Color—All colors equally acceptable with or without dark tips to ears and beard.

The distinctive head of the Lhasa Apso should have a heavy fall of hair over the eyes, as well as a full beard and whiskers.

Body Shape—The length from point of shoulders to point of buttocks longer than height at withers, well ribbed up, strong loin, well-developed quarters and thighs.

Coat—Heavy, straight, hard, not woolly nor silky, of good length, and very dense.

Mouth and Muzzle—The preferred bite is either level or slightly undershot. Muzzle of medium length; a square muzzle is objectionable.

Head—Heavy head furnishings with good fall over eyes, good whiskers and beard; skull narrow, falling away behind the eyes in a marked degree, not quite flat, but not domed or apple-shaped; straight foreface of fair length. Nose black, the length from tip of nose to eye to be roughly about one-third of the total length from nose to back of skull.

Eyes—Dark brown, neither very large and full, nor very small and sunk.

Ears—Pendant, heavily feathered.

Legs—Forelegs straight; both forelegs and hind legs heavily furnished with hair.

Feet—Well feathered, should be round and catlike, with good pads.

Tail and Carriage—Well feathered, should be carried well over back in a screw; there may be a kink at the end. A low carriage of stern is a serious fault.

Approved July 11, 1978

SELECTING the Right Lhasa Apso for You

WHERE TO BUY YOUR LHASA APSO

The Lhasa Apso you buy will live with you for many years to come. It is not at all unusual for the well-bred Lhasa Apso to live into his late teens or even longer. Obviously, it is important that the dog you select has the advantage of beginning life in a healthy environment and comes from sound, healthy stock.

The only way you can be sure of this is to go directly to a breeder who has earned a reputation over the years for consistently producing Lhasa Apsos that are mentally and physically sound. The only way a breeder is able to earn this reputation is by following a well-planned breeding program that has been governed by rigid selectivity. Selective breeding programs are aimed at maintaining the many fine qualities of the Lhasa Apso and eliminating any genetic weaknesses.

This process is both time consuming and costly for a breeder, but it ensures the buyer gets a dog that will be a joy to own. Responsible Lhasa Apso breeders protect their investment by basing their breeding programs on the

Chocolate, vanilla, or strawberry— the Lhasa's coat comes in many different "flavors."

healthiest, most representative stock available and providing each succeeding generation with the very best care and nutrition.

The governing kennel clubs of the world maintain lists of local breed clubs and breeders that can lead a prospective Lhasa Apso buyer to responsible breeders of quality stock. If you are not sure of

It is important that the Lhasa you select has the advantage of starting life in a healthy environment and comes from sound stock.

A happy and healthy Lhasa puppy is a reflection of his breeder's good care. Ch. Fanfair's Lemon Joy with four-week-old Fanfair Tailwind.

where to contact an established Lhasa Apso breeder in your area, we strongly suggest contacting your kennel club for recommendations.

It is very likely that you will be able to find an established Lhasa Apso breeder in your own area. If so, you will be able to visit the breeder, inspect the premises, and, in many cases, see a puppy's parents and other relatives. These breeders are always willing and able to discuss any problems that might exist in the breed and how they should be dealt with.

Prospective owners should inquire about allergies, eye problems, thyroid dysfunction, kidney disease, and hip dysplasia. This is not to indicate that all Lhasas or all Lhasa bloodlines have these problems, but they do exist. Many breeders practice routine health testing and certification of their breeding stock when possible. Breeders who follow this practice assure the buyer that their dog *is* and *will stay* healthy.

The way your Lhasa puppy interacts with his littermates is a good indication of what his personality will be like as he gets older.

Should there be no breeders in your immediate area, you can arrange to have a puppy shipped to you. There are respected breeders throughout the country whom have

shipped puppies to satisfied owners out of state and even to other countries.

Never hesitate to ask the breeder you visit or deal with any questions or to voice concerns you might have relative to owning a Lhasa Apso. You should expect the breeder to ask you a good number of questions as well. Good breeders are just as interested in placing their puppies in a loving and safe environment as you are in obtaining a happy, healthy puppy.

A good Lhasa Apso breeder will want to know if there are young children in the family and what their ages are. They will also want to know if you or your children have ever owned a dog before. The breeder will want to know if you live in an apartment or in a home. If you live in a home, they will want to know if you have a fenced yard and if there will be someone home during the day to attend to a young puppy's needs.

Not all good breeders maintain large kennels. In fact, you are apt to find many Lhasa Apsos come from the homes of small hobby breeders who keep just a few dogs and have litters only occasionally. The names of these people are just as likely to appear on the recommended lists from kennel clubs as from the larger kennels that maintain many dogs. Hobby breeders are equally dedicated to breeding quality Lhasa Apsos and have the distinct advantage of being able to raise their puppies in a home environment with all the accompanying personal attention and socialization.

Make sure the breeder you are dealing with runs a quality facility and that all the puppies are clean, healthy looking, and well taken care of.

Again, it is important that both the buyer and the seller ask questions. We would be highly suspect of a person who is willing to sell you a Lhasa Apso puppy with no questions asked.

RECOGNIZING A HEALTHY PUPPY

Most Lhasa Apso breeders are apt to keep their puppies until they are at least ten weeks of age and have been given all of their puppy inoculations. By the time the litter is eight weeks of age, they are entirely weaned and no longer nursing on their mother. While puppies are nursing, they are given at

least partial immunity from diseases from their mother. Once they have stopped nursing, however, they become highly susceptible to infectious diseases. Several of these diseases can be transmitted on the hands and clothing of humans. Therefore, it is extremely important that your puppy is current on all the shots he must have for his age before he leaves his first home!

SELECTING A PUPPY

A healthy Lhasa Apso puppy is bouncy and playful. Never select a puppy that appears shy or listless because you feel sorry for him. Doing so will undoubtedly lead to heartache and expensive veterinary costs. It is important, however, not to confuse "quiet and reserved" with "shy and listless."

The Lhasa pup you choose should be bouncy, bright-eyed, and interested in the world around him.

Do not attempt to make up for what the breeder did not do in providing proper care and nutrition. It seldom works.

Many puppies are more quiet and reserved by nature and will sit back and watch all the commotion rather than participating. These puppies are not shy at all. They are not frightened and do not run from attention if it is offered. It is simply their nature to be quiet. Shy puppies run away with their tail down, often shivering or crying with fright when picked up. A listless puppy usually has some accompanying physical sign of illness such as diarrhea, fever, and discharge from the eyes, ears, or nose. If one puppy is sick, I would be leery of the whole litter!

Although Lhasa Apso puppies are small, they should feel sturdy to the touch. They should not feel bony, nor should their abdomens be bloated and extended. A puppy that has just eaten may have a full belly, but the puppy should never appear obese.

It's easy to fall in love with an adorable Lhasa puppy. Three-month-old Fanfair's Gummbi Bear, owned by Jan and Larry Bruton, does his part around the yard.

A healthy puppy's ears will be pink and clean. Dark discharge or a bad odor could indicate ear mites, a sure sign of lack of cleanliness and poor maintenance. A Lhasa Apso puppy's breath should always smell sweet. His teeth must be clean and bright and there should never be any malformation of the jaw, lips, or nostrils.

Lhasa Apso eyes are dark and clear. Runny eyes, or eyes that appear red and irritated, could be caused by a myriad of problems, none of which indicate a healthy puppy. The nose should be cold and wet.

Coughing or diarrhea are danger signals, as is any discharge from the nose or eruptions on the skin. The skin should be clean, the coat soft, clean, and lustrous. In fact, the puppy should smell of nothing other than a good shampoo.

Since the Lhasa Apso is a medium-boned breed, young puppies can seem to have "knottier" joints than some other fine-boned breeds. Agility of movement is the best indication of sound structure in a puppy.

Shuffling, rolling heaviness of movement is a telltale sign of future problems. Lean-boned, leggy puppies will often toe out slightly until they mature and it is of no concern. Toeing out in a heavy-boned puppy, however, indicates a serious bow in the foreleg, which is a major problem.

The puppy's attitude tells you a great deal about his state of health. Puppies that are feeling "out of sorts" react very quickly and will usually find a warm littermate to snuggle up to and prefer to stay that way, even when the rest of the gang wants to play or go exploring. Just make sure the puppy is, in fact, not well, and not simply having a quiet moment. The Lhasa Apso puppy is playful and curious. Do not settle for anything less in selecting your puppy.

SELECTING A SHOW-PROSPECT PUPPY

If you or your family are considering a show career for your puppy we strongly advise putting yourself into the hands of an established breeder who has earned a reputation for breeding winning show dogs. They alone are most capable of anticipating what one might expect a young puppy of their line to develop into when he reaches maturity.

Although the potential buyer should read the American Kennel Club standard of perfection for the Lhasa Apso, it is hard for the novice to really understand the nuances of what is being asked for. The experienced breeder is best equipped to do so and will be very happy to assist you in your quest. Even at that, no one can make accurate predictions or guarantees about a very young puppy.

Any predictions a breeder is apt to make are based upon the breeder's experience with past litters that produced winning show dogs. It should be obvious that the more successful a breeder has been in producing winning Lhasa Apsos through the years, the broader his or her basis of comparison will be.

What a natural! Like this little guy owned by Leslie Ann Engen, some puppies are born show dogs.

The most any responsible breeder will say about a puppy is that he has "show potential." If you are serious about showing your Lhasa Apso and want something you feel sure is going to be of championship caliber, most breeders strongly suggest waiting until a Lhasa Apso is old enough to make this determination.

Type

We prefer to see puppies at about eight to ten weeks of age when determining show potential. The first thing we look for is "breed type." The word "type" in purebred dogs means a combination of those things that, in the end, distinguish a dog as the member of its own breed and not of another. The "typey" dog carries a preponderance of those characteristics.

The Lhasa puppy must have a narrow skull; clean almond-shaped eyes set not too far apart. There should be good length of muzzle with no hint of squareness, and the muzzle should be in an approximate 1:2 ratio to the skull. There should be a moderate to shallow stop where the muzzle meets the skull.

At this age, we prefer to see a scissors, or level, bite. A reverse scissors bite may go too far undershot. Nose pigment should be black.

Size and proportion are also important to type. This is an athletic breed that should be neither toy-like nor big, coarse, and heavy. We like to see medium bone with no obvious achondroplasia (a form of dwarfism primarily affecting development of the long bones of the limbs). The Lhasa Apso's body should be around 35percent longer than height measured at the top of the shoulder.

Coat texture is very hard to evaluate at this age. A rule of thumb is the harder the coat as a puppy, the more apt it is to be correct in the end.

Structure and Movement

The Lhasa Apso puppy should move freely and easily with no bounce or roll. Front legs should be straight with balanced angulation of shoulder and rear assemblies. Since angulation will straighten some during the growing stage, we tend to look for a little more angulation in a puppy than we would in an adult.

Tail should be tight over the back, but it may loosen when the puppy is teething. The stifles (knees) should be checked for soundness.

At maturity, given proper size and good weight, bitches will weigh between 11 and 15 pounds and males between 14 and 18 pounds.

There are many "beauty point" shortcomings a Lhasa Apso puppy might have that would in no way interfere with his being a wonderful companion. These include faults such as one or no testicles for a male, or an incorrect topline or tail set. These faults would be serious drawbacks in the show ring and will keep the puppy from ever being a winner. Many of these flaws are such that a beginner in the breed would hardly notice. This is why employing the assistance of a good breeder is so important. Still, the prospective buyer should be at least generally aware of what the Lhasa Apso show puppy should look like.

Socialization with littermates is very important for a well-adjusted Lhasa Apso. This brother and sister seem to get along just fine.

All of the foregoing points regarding soundness and health of the pet puppy apply to the show puppy as well. The show prospect must not only be sound and healthy, he must adhere to the standard of the breed very closely. The complete standard of the breed appears in another section of this book.

A happy, outgoing attitude is an important thing to consider when searching for a show-prospect puppy.

There are a number of other books that can help the newcomer learn more about the Lhasa Apso. The more you know about the history and origin of the breed, the better equipped you will be to see the differences that distinguish the show dog from the pet.

PUPPY OR ADULT?

For the person anticipating a show career for their Lhasa Apso or for someone hoping to become a breeder, the purchase of a young adult provides greater certainty with respect to quality. Even those who simply want a companion could consider the adult dog.

Bringing an adult Lhasa Apso into your home can be very rewarding. Choosing the "finished product" allows you to pick the dog whose personality and habits suit yours from the start. Hopefully, the adult dog has had some house training and should be past the fluctuating hormones of adolescence, along with the accompanying puppy coat shedding stage.

Transferring ownership of an adult Lhasa Apso can be difficult for the dog in some cases because they are so devoted to their people. With just a little patience, they will adapt to their new situation and bond with their new family.

It is important to remember that the Lhasa Apso is such a persistently strong-willed breed. The same rules that apply to the new puppy must apply to the new adult. The adult Lhasa will not hesitate to take advantage of the new owner if he is allowed to do so. Never let a Lhasa Apso establish any behavior that you don't wish to live with for the rest of the dog's life!

We strongly advise taking an adult dog on a trial basis to see if the dog will adapt to the new owner's lifestyle and environment. Most often it works, but on rare occasions a prospective owner decides that training his or her dog from puppyhood is worth the time and effort it requires. If such an arrangement does not work out, the adult dog should be returned to the person from whom it was obtained.

IDENTIFICATION PAPERS AND AGREEMENTS

The purchase of any purebred dog entitles you to three very important documents: a health record that includes an inoculation or "shot" record, a copy of the dog's pedigree, and the registration certificate. Most responsible breeders accompany the sale of one of their dogs with what may be referred to as a sales contract that will include health guarantees, a spay or neuter agreement, and first right of refusal for the breeder in the event the dog is to be sold in the future. Any additional conditions between buyer and breeder should be included in the contract before it is signed in duplicate—one copy for each party.

Inoculations

You will find that most Lhasa Apso breeders have initiated the necessary preliminary inoculation series for their puppies by the time they are 12 weeks of age. These inoculations temporarily protect the puppies against hepatitis, leptospirosis, distemper, and canine parvovirus. Permanent inoculations will follow at a prescribed time. Since different breeders and veterinarians follow different approaches to inoculations, it is extremely important that the health record you obtain for your puppy accurately lists what shots have been given and when. In this way, the veterinarian you choose will be able to continue with the appropriate inoculation series as needed.

In some areas, there are laws that any dog or cat over three months of age must be vaccinated against rabies. Our veterinarian recommends rabies vaccination at about 16 weeks. They must get a booster shot at one year that is then good for three years.

Pedigree

The pedigree is your dog's "family tree." The breeder must supply you with a copy of this document that authenticates your puppy's ancestors back to at least the third generation. All purebred dogs have pedigrees. The pedigree itself does not mean that your puppy is of show quality. It means is that all of his ancestors were, in fact, registered Lhasa Apso. They may all have been of pet quality. Unscrupulous puppy dealers often try to imply that a pedigree indicates that all dogs having one are of championship caliber. This is not true. Again, it simply tells you all of the dog's ancestors are purebred.

The breeder will have started your Lhasa Apso pup on the road to good nutrition, so stick to this same diet when you bring him home.

Registration Certificate

The registration certificate is the canine world's "birth certificate." A country's governing kennel club issues this certificate. When you transfer the ownership of your Lhasa Apso from the breeder's name to your own, the transaction is entered on this certificate and, once mailed to the appropriate kennel club, it is permanently recorded in their computerized files.

Keep all of your dog's documents in a safe place, as you will need them when you visit your veterinarian or should you ever wish to breed or show your Lhasa Apso. Keep the name, address, and phone number of the breeder from whom you purchase your Lhasa Apso in a separate place as well. Should you ever lose any of these important documents, you will then be able to contact the breeder to obtain duplicates.

DIET SHEET

Your Lhasa Apso is the happy, healthy puppy he is because the breeder has carefully fed and cared for him. Every breeder we know has his or her own particular way of doing this. Most breeders give the new owner a written record that details the amount and kind of food a puppy has been receiving. Follow these recommendations to the letter at least for the first month or two after the puppy comes to live with you.

The diet sheet should indicate the number of times a day your Lhasa Apso has been accustomed to being fed and the kind of vitamin supplementation, if any, he has been receiving. Following the prescribed procedure will reduce the chance of upset stomach and loose stools.

Usually, a breeder's diet sheet projects the increases and changes in food that will be necessary as your puppy grows. If the sheet does not include this information, ask the breeder for suggestions regarding increases and the eventual changeover to adult food.

In the unlikely event that you are not supplied with a diet sheet by the breeder and are unable to get one, your veterinarian will be able to advise you in this respect. There are countless foods now being manufactured expressly to meet the nutritional needs of puppies and growing dogs. A trip down the pet aisle at your supermarket will prove just how many choices you have. Two important tips to remember: read labels carefully for content, and when dealing with established, reliable manufacturers, you are more likely to get what you pay for. Feeding and nutrition are dealt with in detail in the chapter on caring for your Lhasa.

HEALTH GUARANTEE

Any reputable breeder should be more than willing to supply a written agreement that the purchase of your Lhasa Apso is contingent upon his passing a veterinarian's examination. Ideally, you will be able to arrange an appointment with your chosen veterinarian right after you have picked up your puppy from the

Play time and socialization with littermates will teach your Lhasa how to interact with other dogs later in life.

Caring for a dog teaches a child responsibility and respect for animals and is a great way to form friendships. Julie plays with her Lhasa buddy, Rico.

breeder and before you take him home. If this is not possible, you should not delay this procedure any longer than 24 hours from the time you take your puppy home.

TEMPERAMENT AND SOCIALIZATION

Temperament is both hereditary and environmental. Poor treatment and lack of proper socialization can ruin inherited good temperament. A Lhasa Apso puppy that comes from shy, nervous, or aggressive stock, or one that exhibits those characteristics himself, will make a poor companion or show dog and should certainly never be bred. Therefore, it is critical that you obtain a happy puppy from a breeder who is determined to produce good temperaments and has taken all the necessary steps to provide the early socialization necessary.

Socialization does not end there, however. Ongoing socialization is definitely a must for this breed! Puppy kindergarten is a great start and owners should make sure they introduce puppies to as many different people and situations as possible during the dog's first year.

Have the puppy handled by strangers. If the puppy's struggles, it is very important that you be firm and teach him that strangers must be tolerated. *Be firm!*

Obedience classes are wonderful for the Lhasa Apso and his owner as they offer both socialization and training experience. Failure to socialize the Lhasa Apso properly as a puppy may cause him to become overly fearful of the outside world.

Your puppy should go everywhere with you—the post office, the market, the shopping mall—wherever. Be prepared to create a stir wherever you go

Take your Lhasa with you wherever you go—the more people he meets, the better socialized he will become.

because the very reason you were attracted to the first Lhasa Apso you met applies to other people as well. Everyone will want to pet your little companion and there is nothing in the world better for him.

Should your puppy back off from a stranger, pick him up and hand him to the person. The young Lhasa Apso must be taught all humans—young and old, short and tall, and of all races—are friends. You are in charge. You must call the shots.

If your Lhasa Apso has a show career in his future, other things in addition to just being handled will have to be taught. All show dogs must learn to have their mouth inspected by the judge. The judge must also be able to check the teeth. This is important for the pet Lhasa as well. It is necessary for their health, and contributes greatly toward owners maintaining the alpha, or dominant, position.

Males must be accustomed to having their testicles touched, as the dog show judge must determine that all male dogs are "complete," which means there are two normal-sized testicles in the scrotum. These inspections must begin in puppyhood and be done on a regular and continuing basis.

THE ADOLESCENT LHASA APSO

The Lhasa Apso is very slow to mature. They are not fully mature, physically or mentally, until about the age of three.

Somewhere between four and seven months, the hormones start to kick in and many puppies go through an insecure period. This can last for several months but usually passes before they turn one year old.

45

At any time from around ten months of age, the lovely puppy coat begins to change. When this happens, mats may occur where new hair growth meets existing hair. While it does not always happen, some dogs are more prone to matting than others. Thorough brushing will only take a few minutes, so it should be done every few days to check on the coat's condition and keep it mat free.

This is also the time many pet owners opt for a trip to the groomer and a cute haircut for the Lhasa puppy. Not many pet owners care to spend the time necessary to keep a Lhasa Apso in full coat, and the clipped coat does not pick up and bring in nearly as much debris from the yard as the long coat does.

It is critical that you attend to grooming sessions regularly during the early months of your puppy's growth. If your Lhasa Apso has been groomed regularly as a puppy, he will have learned that this, regardless of what he might prefer, is a way of life. More grooming instructions are given in another chapter.

Other physical changes will occur during this time as well. Tails can do odd things, and the well-placed and carried tail may suddenly be carried higher while the puppy is teething.

The adolescent Lhasa Apso seems to grow in spurts. What once looked like a nicely balanced puppy may look like he is put together with rubber bands at six to nine months. Usually at maturity, they will regain their balanced proportions.

Food needs change during this growth period. Most Lhasa Apsos seem as if they can never get enough to eat, while there may be an occasional puppy that eats just enough to avoid starving. Think of Lhasa Apso puppies as being as individualistic as children and act accordingly. You must also pay close attention to the dog's appearance and condition, as you do not want a puppy to become overweight or obese.

At eight weeks of age, a Lhasa Apso puppy is eating four meals a day. By the time he is six months old, the puppy can do well on two meals a day, with perhaps a midday snack. If your puppy does not eat the food offered, he is either not hungry or not well. Your dog will eat when he is hungry. If you suspect the dog is not well, a trip to the veterinarian is immediately in order.

Adolescence is also a period when an occasional Lhasa Apso becomes too wary of strangers. These dogs require somewhat more socialization, but some may never feel completely comfortable around strangers. The shy dog is usually very loving and affectionate with his own family, but once outside his front door, the dog will feel he is no longer in a safe environment. Fear biting can occur in some instances if the dog is frightened enough. Visiting the veterinarian or groomer can be traumatic for the dog and nothing less than difficult for the people involved.

Training your dog to accept these situations is very important. He doesn't have to like it, as long as he understands that there are certain things he must accept. These cases are rare, but with patience and understanding, cooperation can be achieved.

This adolescent period is a particularly important one. It is the time your Lhasa Apso must learn all the household and social rules by which he will live for the rest of his life. Your patience and commitment during this time will not only produce a respected canine good citizen, but will forge a bond between the two of you that will grow and ripen into a wonderful relationship.

Your Lhasa may question your authority, but you must provide him with the discipline and guidance he needs to succeed in all his endeavors.

CARING for Your Lhasa Apso

FEEDING AND NUTRITION

he best way to make sure your Lhasa Apso puppy is obtaining the right amount and the correct type of food for his age is to follow the diet sheet provided by the breeder from whom you obtain your puppy. Do your best not to change the puppy's diet and you will be less apt to run into digestive problems and diarrhea. Diarrhea is very serious in young puppies. Puppies with diarrhea can dehydrate very rapidly, causing severe problems and even death.

If it is necessary to change your Lhasa Apso puppy's diet for any reason, it should be done gradually over a period of several meals and a few days. Begin by adding a tablespoon or two of the new food and slowly increase the amount until the meal consists entirely of the new product.

By the time your Lhasa Apso is 10 to 12 months old you can reduce feedings to one, or at the most, two a day. The main meal can be given either in the morning or evening. It is really a matter of choice on your part. There are two important things to remember: feed the main meal at the same time every day, and make sure what you feed is nutritionally complete.

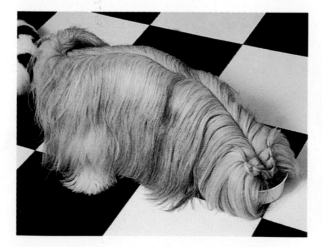

Pick a good-quality dog food that is healthy and appropriate for your Lhasa Apso's age and level of activity.

A morning or nighttime snack of hard dog biscuits made especially for small-sized dogs can supplement the single meal. These biscuits not only become highly anticipated treats, but also are genuinely helpful in maintaining healthy gums and teeth—but do watch those calories!

Make sure your Lhasa has cool clean water available to him at all times.

It is fine to give your Lhasa an occasional treat as long as it is nutritious and does not upset his regular diet. This Lhasa looks like he has helped himself!

Balanced Diets

In order for a canine diet to qualify as "complete and balanced" in the United States, it must meet standards set by the Subcommittee on Canine Nutrition of the National Research Council of the National

Academy of Sciences. Most commercial foods manufactured for dogs meet these standards and prove this by listing the ingredients contained in the food on every package or can. The ingredients are listed in descending order with the main ingredient listed first.

Fed with any regularity at all, refined sugars can cause your Lhasa Apso to become obese and will definitely create tooth decay. Candy stores do not exist in nature and canine teeth are not genetically disposed to handling sugars. Do not feed your Lhasa Apso candy or sweets and avoid products that contain sugar to any high degree.

Fresh water and a properly prepared, balanced diet containing the essential nutrients in correct proportions are all a healthy Lhasa Apso needs to be offered. Dog foods come canned, dry, semi-moist, "scientifically fortified," and "all-natural." A visit to your local supermarket or pet store will reveal how vast an array from which you will be able to select.

It is important to remember that all

There are a number of quality dog foods that can provide the nutrition your Lhasa requires in each stage of life. Puppies need a growth formula.

dogs, whether toy or giant, are carnivorous (meat-eating) animals. While the vegetable content of the Lhasa Apso diet should not be overlooked, a dog's physiology and anatomy are based upon carnivorous food acquisition. Protein and fat are essential to the well-being of your Lhasa Apso. It is important to remember, however, that the Tibetan diet was low in meat content, therefore a moderate protein diet that is low in fat is best for the Lhasa Apso.

Read the list of ingredients on the package of dog food you buy. Animal protein should appear first on the label's list of ingredients. A base of quality kibble to which the meat and even table scraps have been added can provide a nutritious meal for your Lhasa Apso.

Once he leaves his mother, your Lhasa Apso puppy will look to you to fulfill all his nutritional needs.

This having been said, it should be realized in the wild carnivores eat the entire beast they capture and kill. The carnivore's kills consist almost entirely of herbivorous (plant-eating) animals and invariably, the carnivore begins its meal with the contents of the herbivore's stomach. This provides the carbohydrates, minerals, and nutrients present in vegetables.

Through centuries of domestication, we have made our dogs entirely dependent upon us for their well-being. Therefore, we are entirely responsible for duplicating the food balance the wild dog finds in nature. The domesticated dog's diet must include protein, carbohydrates, fats, roughage, and small amounts of essential minerals and vitamins.

Finding commercially prepared diets that contain all the necessary nutrients will not present a problem. It is important to understand though; these commercially prepared foods do contain most of the nutrients your Lhasa Apso requires.

Oversupplementation

A great deal of controversy exists today regarding the orthopedic problems that afflict many breeds. Some claim these problems are entirely hereditary conditions, but many others feel they can be exacerbated by the overuse of mineral and vitamin supplements for puppies. Oversupplementation is now looked upon by some breeders as a major contributor to many skeletal abnormalities found in the purebred dogs of the day. In giving vitamin supplementation, one should *never* exceed the prescribed amount. No vitamin, however, is a substitute for a nutritious, balanced diet.

Pregnant and lactating bitches do require supplementation of some kind, but again it is not a case of "if a little is good, a lot would be a great deal better." Extreme caution is advised in this case and it is best discussed with your veterinarian.

Many Lhasa Apsos will try to convince their owners to supplement their food with tasty bits of table food. This should never be done. It only encourages poor eating habits as well upsetting the balance of the diet and adding unnecessary calories. Owners must be firm no matter how convincing an act their Lhasa Apso puts on!

Dogs do not care if food looks like a hot dog or a piece of cheese. Truly nutritious dog foods are seldom manufactured to look like food that appeals to humans. Dogs only care about how food smells and tastes. It is highly doubtful you will be eating your dog's food, so do not waste your money on these "looks just like" products.

When you establish the basic "building blocks" of training and socialization, your Lhasa will become a well-mannered companion and friend.

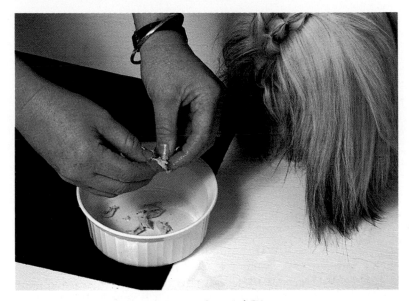

You should only supplement your Lhasa Apso's diet if your veterinarian recommends it.

Special Diets

There are many commercially prepared diets for dogs with special dietary needs. The overweight, underweight, or geriatric dog can have his nutritional needs met, as can puppies and growing dogs. The calorie content of these foods is adjusted accordingly. With the correct amount of the right foods and the proper amount of exercise, your Lhasa Apso should stay in top shape. Again, common sense must prevail. Too many calories will increase weight; too few will reduce weight.

Occasionally, a young Lhasa Apso going through the teething period will become a poor eater. The concerned owner's first response is to tempt the dog by hand-feeding special treats and foods that the problem eater seems to prefer. This practice only serves to compound the problem. Once the dog learns to play the waiting game, he will turn up his nose at anything other than his favorite food, knowing full well that what he *wants* to eat will eventually arrive.

Unlike humans, dogs have no suicidal tendencies. A healthy dog will not starve himself to death. He may not eat enough to keep him in the shape we find ideal and attractive, but he will definitely eat enough to maintain himself. If your Lhasa Apso is not eating properly and appears to be too thin, it is probably best to consult your veterinarian.

SPECIAL NEEDS OF THE LHASA APSO

It is important to remember that the Lhasa Apso comes from a place like no other in the world. Their metabolism was developed through a diet consisting mostly of "tsampa," which is the barley paste that serves as the staple of the Tibetan diet. The dogs did not eat meat on a regular basis, the exception being any vermin they could catch or scavenging the remains of dead carcasses.

Like most dogs, the Lhasa will do almost anything for a treat.

The Lhasa is what dog folk refer to as an "easy keeper." The breed tends to be a hardy, healthy dog and does not require much more than good general canine care. Care must be taken, however, not to let the Lhasa Apso become overweight. The obese dog is prone to so many health problems that it is worth the owner's time to prevent it from happening. Exercise will keep the Lhasa Apso in good physical condition and is not only fun for both dog and owner, but the Lhasa will also have the humans he loves around much longer if they too participate in the exercise program.

Naturally, common sense must be used in the extent and the intensity of the exercise you give your Lhasa Apso. Remember, young puppies have short bursts of energy and then require long rest periods. No puppy of any breed should be forced to accompany you on extended walks. Serious injuries can result. Again—short exercise periods and long rest stops for any Lhasa Apso under 10 or 12 months of age. Most adult Lhasa Apso, however, will willingly walk as far as the average owner is inclined to go.

Puppies need exercise, but they also need plenty of rest. This Lhasa pup is just "flat out" exhausted!

Caution must be exercised in very hot weather. Plan your walks for the first thing in the morning, if possible. If you cannot arrange to do this, wait until the sun has set and the outdoor temperature has dropped to a comfortable degree.

You must *never* leave your Lhasa Apso in a car during hot weather. Temperatures can soar in a matter of minutes and your dog can die of heat exhaustion in less time than you would ever imagine. Rolling down the windows helps little and is dangerous in that an overheated Lhasa Apso will panic and could attempt to escape through the open window. A word to the wise—leave your dog at home in a cool room on hot days.

The Lhasa Apso's long coat requires extensive grooming to keep it in good condition.

The most important thing to remember in guiding your young Lhasa Apso through adolescence is that you are in charge. You make the rules and your Lhasa must follow them!

COAT CARE

Much of what initially attracts people to the Lhasa Apso is his lovely long coat. We wish we could tell you it does not take much to maintain that look. Unfortunately, we can't. Your Lhasa Apso will only have that special show dog look with expertise and diligence; usually far more expertise and diligence than the average pet owner is willing to invest. This does not mean you cannot own a Lhasa Apso. The short pet trims are attractive and easy to manage, and the clipped Lhasa coat is as hypoallergenic as any Poodle's.

The amount of grooming required is dependent upon how the coat is kept and how the owner likes the dog to look. Coat texture is a major consideration if the owner would like to keep the coat long. The proper straight, heavy, and hard coat texture requested in the breed standard is much easier to

Your Lhasa must become accustomed to grooming procedures if he is to compete in the show ring.

maintain than the thick, soft open coats that are so prevalent today.

The Lhasa Apso does shed to some degree. He has a standard canine "double coat," with a long, coarse guard coat on the outside and the soft, downy undercoat next to the skin. The undercoat will shed out twice a year just as the coats of most dogs do, but instead of ending on the floor it gets caught in the long guard coat and causes matting. The harder and straighter the guard coat texture is, the more easily the undercoat slides through and off the dog. The softer the guard hair, the more matting that occurs.

This Lhasa's banded headpiece helps keep his hair out of the dog's food and water.

Regular grooming promotes healthy skin and coat, as well as providing the opportunity to find any burgeoning health problems. Notice should always be taken of any changes in skin, coat, ears, and eyes, and those changes should be discussed with your veterinarian. The Lhasa Apso does prefer to be clean and enjoys looking his best, often acting the real ham after grooming. A Lhasa Apso with the correct coat texture only requires grooming once a week or so to keep it in beautiful condition.

Foxtails and weed seeds tend to catch in the armpits and groin area of the Lhasa Apso. This is the undoubtedly due to their short legs and wealth of coat. They will quickly create an abscess if not removed.

Both inhalant and food allergies can be a problem with the Lhasa Apso. The owner should consider seasonal or dietary changes if problems arise. Dry eye also occurs in this breed. Regular grooming will keep you abreast of any problems developing in these areas.

Owners who do not wish to show their dogs sometimes prefer to keep their Lhasa's coat clipped short, making it easier to care for.

Puppy and Short Coats

Undoubtedly, the breeder from whom you purchased your Lhasa Apso will have accustomed the puppy to grooming just as soon as there was enough hair to brush. You must continue with grooming sessions or begin them at once if for some reason they have not been started. You and your Lhasa Apso will spend considerable time over the months and years involved with this activity, so it is imperative that you both learn to cooperate in the endeavor to make it an easy and pleasant experience.

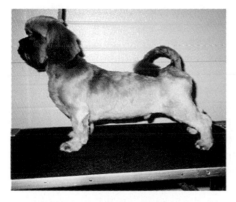

The first piece of equipment you should obtain is a grooming table. A grooming table can be built or purchased at your local pet emporium. Even a sturdy card table topped with a non-skid pad can be used, just so long as it is steady and does not wobble or shake. An unsteady table is a very frightening thing for any dog.

Make sure that whatever kind of table you use, it is of a height at which you can work comfortably. Adjustable-height grooming tables are available at most pet shops.

You will also need to invest in two brushes, a steel comb with medium and fine teeth, barber's scissors, and a pair of nail clippers. Unless you keep your dog's coat extremely short, an electric hair dryer with heat control is necessary. Electric clippers can be useful as well, and we will discuss their value later. Also very useful is a good-quality, spray-type coat conditioner. Consider the fact you will be using these grooming tools for many years to come, so buy the best of these items that you can afford.

The brush that you will need is called a pin brush, sometimes called a "Poodle brush." The other brush you will need is called a slicker brush. All of these supplies can be purchased at your local pet shop or at any dog show.

Do not attempt to groom your puppy on the floor. The puppy will only attempt to get away from you when he has decided that enough is enough, and you will spend a good part of your time chasing the puppy around the room. Nor is sitting on the floor for long stretches of time the most comfortable position in the world for the average adult.

The Lhasa Apso puppy should be taught to lie on his side to be groomed. As your Lhasa Apso grows and develops a heavier adult coat, you will find that the bit of effort you invested in teaching the puppy to lie on his side will be time well spent, as he will be kept in that position for most of the brushing process. Your Lhasa Apso will also have to be kept in the standing position for some of his grooming, but lying on his side is a bit more difficult for the puppy to learn.

Begin this training by laying the puppy down on his side on the table. Pick the puppy up as you would a lamb, hold him to your chest, and lean down with the puppy until he is resting on the table. Speak reassuringly to the puppy, stroking his head and rump. This is a good time to practice the stay

command. Do this a number of times before you attempt to do any grooming. Repeat the process until your puppy understands what he is supposed to do when you place him on the grooming table.

Regular grooming is a great way to keep your Lhasa's coat and skin healthy, as well as keep on top of any coat problems your dog might experience.

The correct Lhasa coat not only protects the dog against the cold, it also acts as insulation in hot weather.

To brush the puppy coat, start with the pin brush. When your Lhasa Apso has developed his adult coat, you will find use for the slicker brush in the heavier, more easily tangled areas of the coat and for overall grooming. Use your fine-toothed comb to help in untangling mats.

Should you encounter a mat that does not brush out easily, use your fingers and the steel comb to help separate the hairs as much as possible. Do not cut or pull out the matted hair. Apply coat conditioner directly to the mat and brush completely from the skin out.

With the puppy standing, do the chest and tail. When brushing, do so gently so as not to break the hair. When brushing on and around the rear legs make sure to give special attention to the area of the anus and genitalia. It is important to be extremely careful when brushing in these areas because they are very sensitive and easily injured.

Use your fine-toothed comb around the face, being very careful not to catch the eye rim or poke the eye.

Nail Trimming

This is a good time to accustom your Lhasa Apso to having his nails trimmed and feet inspected. This can be easier said than done. A Lhasa Apso is typically very sensitive about his feet being touched, particularly the front feet. Care must be taken to teach the Lhasa that he must submit to having his feet taken care of from puppyhood. Untrained dogs will often bite when you try to touch their front feet, so it is very important they be taught from the beginning that this is one of those situations that has nothing to do with what the dog might prefer.

Always inspect your dog's feet for cracked pads. If your Lhasa Apso is allowed out in the yard or accompanies you to the park or woods, check between the toes for splinters and thorns. Pay particular attention to any swollen or tender areas. In many sections of the country there is a weed called a foxtail, which releases a small,

The hair between your Lhasa's pads should be kept short to lessen the chance of your dog slipping or picking up splinters or thorns.

barbed, hook-like affair that carries its seed. This hook easily finds its way into a dog's foot or between his toes and quickly works its way deep into the dog's flesh. This will very quickly cause soreness and infection. These barbs should be removed by your veterinarian before serious problems result.

The nails of a Lhasa Apso who spends most of his time indoors or on grass when outdoors can grow long very quickly. Do not allow the nails to become overgrown and expect to cut them back easily. Each nail has a blood vessel running through the center called the quick, which grows close to the end of the nail and contains very sensitive nerve endings. If the nail is allowed to grow too long, it will be impossible to cut it back to a proper length without cutting into the quick. This causes severe pain to the dog and can also result in a great deal of bleeding that can be very difficult to stop.

Your Lhasa's feet should be inspected regularly for injuries and his toenails kept short to prevent any tearing or discomfort.

Should the quick be nipped in the trimming process, there are any number of blood-clotting products available at pet shops that will almost immediately stem the flow of blood. It is wise to have one of these products on hand in case there is a nail trimming accident or the dog tears a nail on his own.

Grooming the Adult Lhasa Apso

Ideally, you and your Lhasa Apso have spent the many months between puppyhood and full maturity learning to help each other through the grooming process. The two of you have survived the changing of the puppy coat and the arrival of the entirely different adult hair. The hair of the adult Lhasa Apso is more profuse, and if allowed to grow unchecked, will become very long.

The method of brushing the adult coat is the same as that used since your Lhasa Apso was a puppy. The only real difference is that you have a bit more dog and the hair itself will be longer unless you cut it back.

While one might expect grooming an adult Lhasa Apso to be a monumental task, this is not necessarily so. The important thing is consistency. A few minutes a day, every day, precludes your dog's hair from becoming a tangled mess that may take you hours to undo.

If you accustom your Lhasa to being groomed, it will come to be a pleasant experience for both of you.

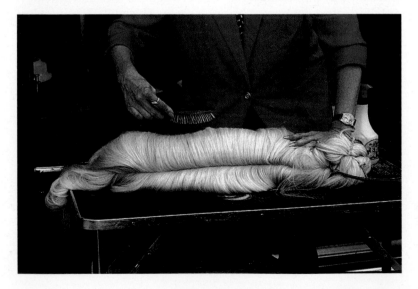

These San-Jo Lhasas owned by Leslie Ann Engen have their long furnishings banded between dog shows.

Then, too, the two of you have been practicing the brushing routine for so long that it has undoubtedly become second nature to both of you.

Some owners find the long flowing coat particularly attractive and wish to keep it that way at all times. This, of course, is an absolute necessity if the dog is to be shown. Maintaining a show coat is not for the novice, and we strongly suggest you consult the breeder from whom you purchased your Lhasa Apso or an experienced professional groomer.

Most pet owners find that maintaining the long coat is an extremely demanding task and use scissors to cut the coat back to a manageable length. Electric clippers can be used to remove the hair from the frequently matted armpits (under the legs where they join the body) and under the dog's stomach.

If you do not care to keep the coat long, a Lhasa Apso can be kept in a very cute "puppy trim." The body is trimmed with the electric clippers using a No. 4 blade. The ears, whiskers, and tail are left longer to maintain the distinctive Lhasa Apso look.

Be sure to rinse your dog's coat thoroughly after bathing to remove all shampoo residue. Ch. San Jo Dressed To The Nines takes his weekly bath.

Hair should be removed from between the toe pads. You can use barber scissors or electric clippers to accomplish this.

It is important to note that Lhasa coat color can change periodically. This is the case even with the completely matured adult coat. The coat color is affected by general health, hormones, time of the year, and diet. Any abrupt physiological changes can result in a "rainbow" appearance of the coat, with horizontal stripes of light and dark shades of color. The changes will not last long, so the effect can be quite striking while in progress.

BATHING

Bathe your Lhasa only when needed. Depending upon the lifestyle of the dog, some will need a bath every two or three weeks, while others may go a month or more. Use a quality shampoo made especially for dogs. Use caution here—a Lhasa

Apso should never be bathed until after it has been thoroughly brushed. If all mats are not out before you bathe, you will end up with a fused cotton ball! Mats will only get worse when doused with water.

A small cotton ball placed inside each ear will prevent water from running down into the dog's ear canal, and a drop or two of mineral oil or a dab of petroleum jelly placed around the rim of each eye will preclude shampoo irritation.

Everybody in! This Lhasa's affection for his baby pool will surely make bath time a snap.

A rubber mat should be placed at the bottom of the tub so that your dog does not slip and become frightened. A rubber spray hose is necessary to remove all shampoo residue. Rinse thoroughly, apply a quality coat conditioner, and rinse again.

In bathing, start behind the ears and work back. Finally, wash around the face, being very careful not to get suds in your dog's eyes. Rinse well. Shampoo residue in the coat is sure to dry the hair and could cause skin irritation.

As soon as you have completed the bath, use a heavy towel to remove as much of the excess water as possible. Your Lhasa Apso will undoubtedly assist you in the process by shaking a great deal of the water out of the coat on his own.

If you do use a hair dryer while brush-drying your dog, it is very important to use your brush gently and set your hair dryer at medium setting, never hot. The hot setting will not only dry out the hair but also could seriously burn the skin of your dog.

Keep the ears clean by putting in a little ear cleanser and wiping with a tissue. Do not probe into the ear beyond where you can see! The delicate eardrum can be easily injured. If you suspect a problem further down in the ear canal, consult your veterinarian.

HOUSEBREAKING and Training Your Lhasa Apso

I n addition to the normal good manners that every puppy needs to learn, the very possessive and territorial tendencies of the Lhasa Apso demand that owners create special training situations to address these potential problems. Between three and four months of age, the typical Lhasa Apso will begin to challenge your authority. If puppy owners counter these initial skirmishes with absolute firmness, they will have the beginnings of a wonderful and rewarding relationship with their Lhasa Apso.

If, however, these tests by the puppy are met with only soft entreaties to behave or even worse, giggles and laughter at the puppy's spunk, it could be the start of an escalating pattern of canine tyranny. It is absolutely essential, therefore, that puppy owners take some extra time and make a point of teaching the puppy to allow items to be taken away from him, to be moved aside from his place on the sofa or bed, and lie quietly on his back without struggling. These lessons are non-negotiable and owners should practice them on a daily basis with the puppy in order to set the ground rules for the rest of the dog's life.

The intelligent and devoted Lhasa Apso is very trainable using the correct methods.

Toys and chew bones should be taken out of the puppy's mouth and food bowls deliberately touched and taken away by the owner while the puppy is eating. When the object is given up without protest, the puppy should be praised warmly and given back the object. The owner should quickly and firmly discourage any defensive postures or aggressive actions by the puppy.

A Lhasa Apso puppy should never be allowed to keep an object after it has warned the owner away. The object should be taken gently but firmly from the puppy's mouth and the appropriate correction given for the offense. That correction could range from a low verbal warning for offenses like the puppy's merely clenching his teeth and refusing to let go to a pinch or a shaking and loud scolding for growling or snapping.

Praise should always be given after the item is taken away. This lesson should be repeated until the puppy knows that he

has no choice in the matter and dares not challenge anyone if they come near his possessions.

Putting the puppy in a submissive position, such as on his back, and teaching the puppy to lie on his side during grooming sessions is an important part of the owner's maintaining the alpha position in the relationship. Puppy rebellions can be loud, prolonged, and very unpleasant, but the owner must persist until the puppy relents—and they always do.

Tone of voice is very important in training a Lhasa Apso—far more important than most people realize. The Lhasa Apso is especially sensitive to tone of voice. If you are too soft spoken with your reprimands, the dog will assume he has your permission to resume whatever activity for which your were "praising" him. Never say, "no, no" in a tone of voice that can be interpreted by the Lhasa Apso to mean "yes, yes."

If these simple lessons are taught properly, it will go a long way toward establishing a healthy and happy relationship between the Lhasa Apso and his owner. It is much easier to prevent a behavior problem from developing in the puppy than to retrain an adult dog that has become accustomed to behaving in a manner the dog has decided is suitable. Simply ignoring undesirable behavior, as is suggested by some dog trainers, is considered by the Lhasa Apso to be approval of their actions. Dominant aggression is unfortunately a common problem seen in this breed, sadly evidenced by the large number of Lhasa Apsos being turned over to shelters and rescue organizations, as well as those euthanized by veterinarians. In fact, many of these poor dogs' behavior problems could have been prevented through proper early discipline. Owners must take a pro-active role if they want their Lhasa Apso puppy to be a well-mannered companion that will be a joy to live with and love.

HOUSEBREAKING

The Crate Method

Housebreaking is normally very easy with the Lhasa Apso if the puppy has had a good foundation with the breeder. Puppies who have never learned to tolerate unsanitary conditions will be easy to keep from doing so. It is important for the owner to remember, however, the major key to successfully training your Lhasa Apso, whether it is obedience training or housebreaking, is *avoidance*. Crate training is a highly successful method of housebreaking and helps to avoid bad habits before they begin.

First-time dog owners are inclined to initially see the crate method of housebreaking as cruel, but those same people will return later and thank us profusely for having suggested it in the first place. They are also surprised to find that the puppy will eventually come to think of his crate as a place of private retreat—a den, to which he will go for rest and privacy. The success of the crate method is based upon the fact that puppies will not soil the area in which they sleep unless they are forced.

Just like babies, puppies have short attention spans. With persistence, praise, and repetition, however, they will learn what you have to teach them.

Use of a crate reduces housetraining time to an absolute minimum and avoids keeping a puppy under constant stress by incessantly correcting him for making mistakes in the house. The anti-crate advocates consider it cruel to confine a puppy for any length of time, but find no problem in constantly harassing and punishing the puppy because he has wet on the carpet or relieved himself behind the sofa.

Crates come in a variety of styles. The fiberglass shipping kennels used by many airlines are popular with many Lhasa Apso owners, but residents of the extremely warm climates sometimes prefer the wire cage type. Both are available at pet stores.

Your Lhasa Apso will soon come to think of his crate as a cozy place in which to retreat and relax.

The crate used for housebreaking should only be large enough for the puppy to stand, lie down, and stretch out comfortably. If the crate is too large, the puppy will sleep at one end and relieve himself at the other. There are many sizes to choose from. We advise using the No. 200 fiberglass or No. 202 wire-type crate. The former is constructed of fiberglass and the size seems ideal for most full-grown Lhasa Apsos.

Begin to feed your Lhasa Apso puppy in the crate. Keep the door closed and latched while the puppy is eating. When the meal is finished, open the cage and *carry* the puppy outdoors to the spot where you want him to learn to eliminate. If you consistently take your puppy to the same spot, you will reinforce the habit of going there for that purpose. In the event you do not have outdoor access or will be away from home for long periods of time, begin housebreaking by placing newspapers in some out of the way corner that is easily accessible for the puppy.

Crate training is the fastest and easiest way to housebreak your Lhasa Apso.

It is important that you do not let the puppy loose after eating. Young puppies will eliminate almost immediately after eating or drinking. They will also be ready to relieve themselves when they first wake up and after playing. If you keep a watchful eye on your puppy you will quickly learn when this is about to take place. A puppy usually circles and sniffs the floor just before he relieves himself. Do not give your puppy an opportunity to learn that he can eliminate in the house! Your housetraining chores will be reduced considerably if you avoid this happening in the first place.

If you are not able to watch your puppy every minute, he should be in his crate with the door securely latched. Each time you put your puppy in the crate, give him a small treat of some kind. Throw the treat to the back of the crate and encourage the puppy to walk in on his own. When he does so, praise him and perhaps hand him another piece of the treat through the opening in the front of the crate.

Most dogs are good about going into the crate, but many will not readily come *out!* Never reach in to grab and pull the puppy out. Always encourage the puppy to come out on his own and praise him warmly when he does.

Do not succumb to your puppy's complaints about being in his crate. The puppy must learn to stay there and do so without unnecessary complaining. A quick no command and a tap on the crate will usually get the puppy to understand that his theatrics will not result in liberation. Remember that as the pack leader, you make the rules and the puppy is seeking to learn what they are!

Do understand that a puppy of 8 to 12 weeks will not be able to contain himself for long periods. Puppies of that age must relieve themselves every few hours except at night. Your schedule must be adjusted accordingly. Also make sure your puppy has relieved himself—bowel and bladder—the last thing at night and do not dawdle when you wake up in the morning.

Keeping your dog on a regular eating, sleeping, and outdoor schedule is an important key to housebreaking your Lhasa.

Your first priority in the morning is to get the puppy outdoors. Just how early this ritual will take place will depend much more upon your puppy than upon you. If your Lhasa Apso is like most others, there will be no doubt in your mind when he needs to be let out. You will also very quickly learn to tell the difference between the "this is an emergency" complaint and the "I just want out" grumbling. Do not test the young puppy's ability to contain himself. His vocal demand to be let out is confirmation that the housebreaking lesson is being learned.

Should you find it necessary to be away from home all day, you will not be able to leave your puppy in a crate. On the other hand, do not make the mistake of allowing him to roam the house, or even a large room, at will. Confine the puppy to a very small

Home sweet home! Eight-week-old Fanfair's Supermodel is beginning to appreciate the comforts of her crate.

room or partitioned area and cover the floor with newspaper. We suggest a two-by-three-foot or three-by-three-foot puppy pen as an enclosure. This size area is large enough so that the puppy will not have to relieve himself next to his bed, food, or water bowl.

Lhasas hate to get their feet wet, so rainy weather can prove to be a housetraining problem for the puppy and even the adult. If an outdoor area can be covered for the Lhasa to relieve himself, you will save yourself a lot of aggravation. If this is not possible, using the paper training method is undoubtedly the only route to follow.

BASIC TRAINING

Training the Lhasa Apso for obedience can be quite a challenge. Because it is such an exceptionally intelligent breed, Lhasas are inclined to want to decide things for themselves. Their first response to a given command can be "make me!"

If, however, the right dog is matched with the right owner who employs the right training methods, the sky is the limit. The key, of course, is in finding the right method for your own dog, as Lhasa Apsos are all so uniquely individual in their lookout on life. There are some important basics that all owners must endeavor to teach their Lhasa both for their own sanity and their dog's safety.

The No Command

There is no doubt whatsoever that one of the most important commands your Lhasa Apso puppy will ever learn is the meaning of the no command. It is critical that the puppy learns this command as soon as possible. One important piece of advice in using this and all other commands—*never give a command you are not prepared and able to enforce!* A good leader does not enforce rules arbitrarily. The only way a puppy learns to obey commands is to realize that once issued, commands must be complied with. Learning the no command should start on the first day of the puppy's arrival at your home.

Be fair to your Lhasa Apso. He can easily learn the difference between things he can and cannot do. In a Lhasa's mind, if there are some things that can be done one time that means they can be done *all* of the time.

Leash Training

Begin leash training by putting a soft, lightweight collar on your puppy. After a few hours of occasional scratching at the unaccustomed addition, your puppy will quickly forget it is even there.

It may not be necessary for the puppy or adult Lhasa Apso to wear his collar and identification tags within the confines of your home later, but no Lhasa Apso should ever leave home without a collar and without the attached leash held securely in your hand.

Get your puppy accustomed to his collar by leaving it on for a few minutes at a time. Gradually extend the time you leave the collar on. Once this is accomplished, attach a lightweight leash to the collar while you are playing with the puppy. Do not try to guide the puppy at first. You are only trying to get the puppy used to having something attached to the collar.

Every puppy can benefit from basic obedience training to teach him how to become a well-mannered housepet.

Coax your puppy along with a treat of some kind to get him to follow you as you move around. Let the puppy smell what you have in your hand and then move a few steps back, holding the treat in front of the puppy's nose. Just as soon as the puppy takes a few steps toward you, praise him enthusiastically and continue to do so as you continue to move along. This method works best outside of the puppy's home environment. Take the puppy to a park or an unfamiliar place where he will be more inclined to look to you for guidance and security.

Make the first few lessons brief and fun for the puppy. Continue the lessons in your home or yard until the puppy is completely unconcerned about the fact that he is on a leash. With a treat in one hand and the leash in the other, you can begin to use both to guide the puppy in the direction you wish

If you take your Lhasa pup to the same place every time to eliminate, he will soon know what is expected of him.

to go. Eventually, the two of you can venture out on the sidewalk in front of your house and then on to adventures everywhere! This is one lesson no puppy is too young to learn.

One should never grab or rush at the puppy to pick him up or correct him. Puppies will learn to run from the owner or cringe submissively, neither of which is desirable. Owners should make a habit of quietly bending to pick the puppy up at odd moments during the day, then just praising him and putting him back down. This promotes confidence that being approached and picked up by people is a normal and pleasant experience for the puppy and not to be feared.

The Come Command

The next most important lesson for the Lhasa Apso puppy to learn is to come when called, therefore it is very important that the puppy learn his name as soon as possible. Constant repetition is what does the trick in teaching a puppy his name.

Use the name every time you talk to your puppy. Talk to your dog? There is a quotation we particularly like that appeared in an old British dog book we found regarding conversations with our canine friends. It states simply: "Of course you should talk to your dogs. But talk sense!"

Learning to come on command could save your dog's life when the two of you venture out into the world. Your dog's response to his name and the word "come" should always be associated with a pleasant experience, such as great praise and petting or even a food treat.

All Lhasa Apsos must learn how to walk on a leash without tugging or pulling.

Again, remember that it is much easier to avoid the establishment of bad habits than it is to correct them once set. *Never* give your Lhasa the come command unless you are sure your puppy will come to you.

The very young puppy is far more inclined to respond to the come command than the older dog. Young Lhasa puppies are inclined to be more dependent upon you than an older dog, so start your come-on-command training early on.

Use the command initially when the puppy is already on his way to you, or give the command while walking or running away from the youngster. Clap your hands and sound very happy and excited about having the puppy join in on this "game."

You may want to attach a long leash or light rope to the puppy's collar to ensure the correct response. Do not chase or punish your puppy for not obeying the come command. Doing so in the initial stages of training makes the youngster associate the command with something to fear and this will result in avoidance rather than the immediate positive response you desire. It is imperative that you praise your Lhasa Apso puppy and give him a treat when he does come to you, even if he voluntarily delays responding for many minutes.

The Sit and Stay Commands

Just as important to your Lhasa Apso puppy's safety as the no command and learning to come when called are the sit and stay commands. Even a very young Lhasa Apso can learn the sit command quickly, especially if it appears to be a game and a food treat is involved.

First, remember that the Lhasa Apso-in-training should always be on collar and leash for all his lessons. A Lhasa Apso puppy is curious about everything and does not particularly care whether he learns the lesson you are trying to teach him.

Give the sit command just before you reach down and exert pressure on your puppy's rear. Praise the puppy profusely when he does sit, although you made the effort. A food treat of some kind always seems to make the experience that much more enjoyable for the puppy.

Continue holding the dog's rear end down and repeat the sit command several times. If your puppy attempts to get up, repeat

Even a very young Lhasa Apso has a great capacity to learn. Keep initial lessons short and always remember to give lots of praise and affection.

the command again while exerting pressure on the rear end until the correct position is assumed. Make your puppy stay in this position a little bit longer with each succeeding lesson. Begin with a few seconds and increase the time as lessons progress over the following weeks.

Once your puppy has mastered the sit lesson, you may start on the stay command. With your Lhasa Apso on leash and facing you, command him to sit, then take a step or two back. If your dog attempts to get up to follow firmly say, "sit, stay!" While you are saying this, raise your hand, palm toward the dog, and again command, "stay!"

This ten-week-old Lhasa pup works on sitting still. For puppies, that's the hardest part!

If your dog attempts to get up, you must correct him at once, returning him to the sit position and repeating, "stay!" Once your Lhasa Apso begins to understand what you want, you can gradually increase the distance you step back. With a long leash attached to your dog's collar, start with a few steps and gradually increase the distance to several yards. It is important for your Lhasa Apso to learn that the sit and stay commands must be obeyed, no matter how far away you are. With advanced training your Lhasa Apso can be taught that the command is to be obeyed even when you leave the room or are entirely out of sight.

As your Lhasa Apso becomes accustomed to responding to this lesson and is able to remain in the sit position for as long as you command, do not end the command by calling the dog to you. Walk back to your Lhasa Apso and say, "OK." This will let your dog know the command is over. You can call the dog to you when your Lhasa Apso becomes entirely dependable.

The sit and stay commands can take considerable time and patience to get across to puppies. You must not forget that their attention span will be short. Keep the stay part of the lesson very short until your puppy is about six months old.

TRAINING CLASSES

There are few limits to what a patient, firm Lhasa Apso owner can teach his or her dog. Lhasa Apsos are highly trainable, but they are also highly determined to have their own way. Once lessons are accepted and mastered, you will find a Lhasa Apso can perform with enthusiasm and gusto that makes all the hard work worthwhile.

For more advanced obedience work beyond the basics, it is wise for the Lhasa Apso owner to consider local professional assistance, particularly with trainers who have had experience in training Lhasas. Many professional trainers have had long-standing experience in avoiding the pitfalls of obedience training and can help you to avoid them as well.

This training assistance can be obtained in many ways. Classes are particularly good in that your dog will learn to obey commands in spite of all the interesting sights and smells of other dogs. There are free-of-charge classes at many parks and recreation facilities, as well as formal and sometimes very expensive individual lessons with private trainers.

Lhasa Apsos make it a point to listen only to those people who make them listen, so having only a trainer work with a Lhasa is particularly useless. Owners must train the Lhasa Apso themselves if there is to be any benefit for either. The rapport that develops between the owner who has trained his or her Lhasa and the dog himself is incomparable. The effort you expend in teaching your dog to be a pleasant companion and good canine citizen pays off in years of enjoyable companionship.

VERSATILITY

There is no end to the number of activities you and your Lhasa Apso can enjoy together. The breed can be highly successful in both conformation shows and obedience trials.

Owners not inclined toward competitive events might find enjoyment in having their Lhasa Apso serve as therapy dogs. Dogs used in this area

Talent times three—these Lhasa Apso pups have the potential to become excellent companions and show dogs—with a little help from their owner, of course!

The versatility of the Lhasa is amazing. Ch. Anbara Mor-Knoll Rani Sonnet is shown here appearing as "Chowsie" in a stage production of Gypsy.

are trained to assist the sick, the elderly, and often the handicapped.

The Lhasa Apso's remarkable empathic abilities make it a breed well suited for therapy work. The well-trained and well-socialized Lhasa Apso seems to instinctively know the emotional needs of the people he visits. His furry little face can coax a smile from almost anyone, and it can be so rewarding to see the comfort he brings just by sitting on a lap and being stroked. He will show off with tricks or just offer kisses and sad eyes.

The thing to remember about Lhasa Apsos is that they each have a special role that they play. It is just that they are the ones who choose that role, not us. Each usually has something at which that he is incredibly good, but it is impossible to predict what it will be. We have a ball player that absolutely astounds us with her talent. It was her idea from the start and we could never have trained her to play ball in a million years!

There is no doubt that Lhasa Apsos are what they are. Although you can only encourage or discourage their existing tendencies, they are a truly unique and wonderful breed. Just ask any person who is owned by one!

SPORT of Purebred Dogs

Welcome to the exciting and sometimes frustrating sport of dogs. No doubt you are trying to learn more about dogs or you wouldn't be deep into this book. This section covers the basics that may entice you, further your knowledge and help you to understand the dog world.

Dog showing has been a very popular sport for a long time and has been taken

Author Nancy Plunkett winning Best of Breed with Ch. Tabu's CL Prime News, CGC.

quite seriously by some. Others only enjoy it as a hobby.

The Kennel Club in England was formed in 1859, the American Kennel Club was established in 1884 and the Canadian Kennel Club was formed in 1888. The purpose of these clubs was to register purebred dogs and maintain their Stud Books. In the beginning, the concept of registering dogs was not readily accepted. More than 36 million dogs have been enrolled in the AKC Stud Book since its inception in 1888. Presently the kennel clubs not only register dogs but adopt and enforce rules and regulations governing dog shows, obedience trials and field trials. Over the years they have fostered and encouraged interest in the health and welfare of the purebred dog. They routinely donate funds to veterinary research for study on genetic disorders.

Below are the addresses of the kennel clubs in the United States, Great Britain and Canada.

Successful showing requires dedication and preparation, but most of all it should be enjoyable for both dogs and handlers alike.

The American Kennel Club
51 Madison Avenue
New York, NY 10010
(Their registry is located at: 5580 Centerview Drive, STE 200, Raleigh, NC 27606-3390)

The Kennel Club
1 Clarges Street
Piccadilly, London, WIY 8AB, England

The Canadian Kennel Club
111 Eglinton Avenue
East Toronto, Ontario M6S 4V7
Canada

Today there are numerous activities that are enjoyable for both the dog and the handler. Some of the activities include conformation showing, obedience competition, tracking, agility, the Canine Good Citizen Certificate, and a wide range of instinct tests that vary from breed to breed. Where you start depends upon your goals which early on may not be readily apparent.

PUPPY KINDERGARTEN

Every puppy will benefit from this class. PKT is the foundation for all future dog activities from conformation to

Well-trained dogs that have been properly socialized will enjoy each other's company.

"couch potatoes." Pet owners should make an effort to attend even if they never expect to show their dog. The class is designed for puppies about three months of age with graduation at approximately five months of age. All the puppies will be in the same age group and, even though some may be a little unruly, there should not be any real problem. This class will teach the puppy some beginning obedience. As in all obedience classes the owner learns how to train his own dog. The PKT class gives the puppy the opportunity to interact with other puppies in the same age group and exposes him to strangers, which is very

Attending puppy kindergarten is not only a great way to teach your Lhasa basic obedience, it is also a perfect place to socialize your puppy with other dogs.

The glamorous life! This quartet of Lhasa Apsos shows the beauty and grace that makes them such naturals in the show ring.

important. Some dogs grow up with behavior problems, one of them being fear of strangers. As you can see, there can be much to gain from this class.

There are some basic obedience exercises that every dog should learn. Some of these can be started with puppy kindergarten.

CONFORMATION

Conformation showing is our oldest dog show sport. This type of showing is based on the dog's appearance—that is his structure, movement and attitude. When considering this type of showing, you need to be aware of your breed's standard and be able to evaluate your dog compared to that standard. The breeder of your puppy or other experienced breeders would be good sources for such an evaluation. Puppies can go through lots of changes over a period of time. Many puppies start out as promising hopefuls and then after maturing may be disappointing as show candidates. Even so this should not deter them from being excellent pets.

Usually conformation training classes are offered by the local kennel or obedience clubs. These are excellent places for training puppies. The puppy should be able to walk on a lead before entering such a class. Proper ring procedure and technique for posing (stacking) the dog will be demonstrated as well as gaiting the dog. Usually certain patterns are used in the ring such as the triangle or the "L." Conformation class, like the PKT class, will give your youngster the opportunity to socialize with different breeds of dogs and humans too.

It takes some time to learn the routine of conformation showing. Usually one starts at the puppy matches that may be AKC Sanctioned or Fun Matches. These matches are generally for puppies from two or three months to a year old, and there may be classes for the adult over the age of 12 months. Similar to point shows, the classes are divided by sex and after completion of the classes in that breed or variety, the class winners compete for Best of Breed or Variety. The winner goes on to compete in the Group and the Group winners compete for Best in Match. No championship points are awarded for match wins.

A few matches can be great training for puppies even though there is no intention to go on showing. Matches enable

the puppy to meet new people and be handled by a stranger—
the judge. It is also a change of environment, which broadens
the horizon for both dog and handler. Matches and other dog
activities boost the confidence of the handler and especially
the younger handlers.

Earning an AKC championship is built on a point system,
which is different from Great Britain. To become an AKC
Champion of Record the dog must earn 15 points. The number
of points earned each time depends upon the number of dogs
in competition. The number of points available at each show
depends upon the breed, its sex and the location of the show.
The United States is divided into
ten AKC zones. Each zone has its
own set of points. The purpose of
the zones is to try to equalize the
points available from breed to
breed and area to
area.The AKC adjusts
the point scale annually.

*In conformation, your
Lhasa will be judged on
how closely he conforms to
the standard of the breed.*

The number of points
that can be won at a
show are between one
and five. Three-, four-
and five-point wins are
considered majors. Not
only does the dog need
15 points won under
three different judges,
but those points must
include two majors
under two different judges. Canada also works on a point
system but majors are not required.

Dogs always show before bitches. The classes available to
those seeking points are: Puppy (which may be divided into 6
to 9 months and 9 to 12 months); 12 to 18 months; Novice;
Bred-by-Exhibitor; American-bred; and Open. The class
winners of the same sex of each breed or variety compete
against each other for Winners Dog and Winners Bitch. A
Reserve Winners Dog and Reserve Winners Bitch are also
awarded but do not carry any points unless the Winners win is
disallowed by AKC. The Winners Dog and Bitch compete with

the specials (those dogs that have attained championship) for Best of Breed or Variety, Best of Winners and Best of Opposite Sex. It is possible to pick up an extra point or even a major if the points are higher for the defeated winner than those of Best of Winners. The latter would get the higher total from the defeated winner.

At an all-breed show, each Best of Breed or Variety winner will go on to his respective Group and then the Group winners will compete against each other for Best in Show. There are seven Groups: Sporting, Hounds, Working, Terriers, Toys, Non-Sporting and Herding. Obviously there are no Groups at speciality shows (those shows that have only one breed or a show such as the American Spaniel Club's Flushing Spaniel Show, which is for all flushing spaniel breeds).

Earning a championship in England is somewhat different since they do not have a point system. Challenge Certificates are awarded if the judge feels the dog is deserving regardless of the number of dogs in competition. A dog must earn three Challenge Certificates under three different judges, with at least one of these Certificates being won after the age of 12 months. Competition is very strong and entries may be higher than they are in the U.S. The Kennel Club's Challenge Certificates are only available at Championship Shows.

In England, The Kennel Club regulations require that certain dogs, Border Collies and Gundog breeds, qualify in a working capacity (i.e., obedience or field trials) before becoming a full Champion. If they do not qualify in the working aspect, then they are designated a Show Champion, which is equivalent to the AKC's Champion of Record. A Gundog may be granted the title of Field Trial Champion (FT Ch.) if it passes all the tests in

Lhasas that compete in the show ring have to become accustomed to extensive traveling.

the field but would also have to qualify in conformation before becoming a full Champion. A Border Collie that earns the title of Obedience Champion (Ob Ch.) must also qualify in the conformation ring before becoming a Champion.

An-Ji's Summer Secret, owned by Angie Jordan, is not only a conformation champion, but also a beloved friend.

The U.S. doesn't have a designation full Champion but does award for Dual and Triple Champions. The Dual Champion must be a Champion of Record, and either Champion Tracker, Herding Champion, Obedience Trial Champion or Field Champion. Any dog that has been awarded the titles of Champion of Record, and any two of the following: Champion Tracker, Herding Champion, Obedience Trial Champion or Field Champion, may be designated as a Triple Champion.

The shows in England seem to put more emphasis on breeder judges than those in the U.S. There is much competition within the breeds. Therefore the quality of the individual breeds should be very good. In the United States we tend to have more "all around judges" (those that judge multiple breeds) and use the breeder judges at the specialty shows. Breeder judges are more familiar with their own breed since they are actively breeding that breed or did so at one time. Americans emphasize Group and Best in Show wins and promote them accordingly.

The shows in England can be very large and extend over several days, with the Groups being scheduled on different days. Though multi-day shows are not common in the U.S., there are cluster shows, where several different clubs will use the same show site over consecutive days.

Westminster Kennel Club is our most prestigious show although the entry is limited to 2500. In recent years, entry has been limited to Champions. This show is more formal than the majority of the shows with the judges wearing formal attire and the handlers fashionably dressed. In most instances the quality of the dogs is superb. After all, it is a show of Champions. It is a good show to study the AKC registered breeds and is by far the most exciting—especially since it is televised! WKC is one of the few shows in this country that is still benched. This means the dog must be in his benched area during the show hours except when he is being groomed, in the ring, or being exercised.

Typically, the handlers are very particular about their appearances. They are careful not to wear something that will detract from their dog but will perhaps enhance it. American ring procedure is quite formal compared to that of other countries. There is a certain etiquette expected between the judge and exhibitor and among the other exhibitors. Of course it is not always the case but the judge is supposed to be polite, not engaging in small talk or acknowledging how well he knows the handler. There is a more informal and relaxed atmosphere at the shows in other countries. For instance, the dress code is more casual. I can see where this might be more fun for the exhibitor and especially for the novice. The U.S. is very handler-oriented in many of the breeds. It is true, in most instances, that the experienced professional handler can present the dog better and will have a feel for what a judge likes.

In England, Crufts is The Kennel Club's own show and is most assuredly the largest dog show in the world. They've been known to have an entry of nearly 20,000, and the show lasts four days. Entry is only gained by qualifying through winning in specified classes at another Championship Show. Westminster is strictly conformation, but Crufts exhibitors and spectators enjoy not only conformation but obedience, agility and a multitude of exhibitions as well. Obedience was admitted in 1957 and agility in 1983.

If you are handling your own dog, please give some consideration to your apparel. For sure the dress code at matches is more informal than the point shows. However, you should wear something a little more appropriate than beach attire or ragged jeans and bare feet. If you check out the handlers and see what is presently fashionable, you'll catch on. Men usually dress with a shirt and tie and a nice sports coat. Whether you are male or female, you will want to wear comfortable clothes and shoes. You need to be able to run with your dog and you certainly don't want to take a chance of falling and hurting yourself. Heaven forbid, if nothing else, you'll upset your dog. Women usually wear a dress or two-piece outfit, preferably with pockets to carry bait, comb, brush, etc. In this case men are the lucky ones with all their pockets. Ladies, think about where your dress will be if you need to kneel on the floor and also think about running. Does it allow freedom to do so?

You need to take along dog; crate; ex pen (if you use one); extra newspaper; water pail and water; all required grooming equipment, including hair dryer and extension cord; table; chair for you; bait for dog and lunch for you and friends; and, last but not least, clean up materials, such as plastic bags, paper towels, and perhaps a bath towel and some shampoo—just in case. Don't forget your entry confirmation and directions to the show.

Anbara's Bo-Jangles, CD, owned by Barbara Wood, is a canine celebrity—she has appeared on television shows and in magazines.

If you are showing in obedience, then you will want to wear pants. Many of our top obedience handlers wear pants that are color-coordinated with

their dogs. The philosophy is that imperfections in the black dog will be less obvious next to your black pants.

Whether you are showing in conformation, Junior Showmanship or obedience, you need to watch the clock and be sure you are not late. It is customary to pick up your conformation armband a few minutes before the start of the class. They will not wait for you and if you are on the show grounds and not in the ring, you will upset everyone. It's a little more complicated picking up your obedience armband if you show later in the class. If you have not picked up your armband and they get to your number, you may not be allowed to show. It's best to pick up your armband early, but then you may show earlier than expected if other handlers don't pick up. Customarily all conflicts should be discussed with the judge prior to the start of the class.

The time spent together on training helps to develop a close bond between dog and owner.

Junior Showmanship

The Junior Showmanship Class is a wonderful way to build self confidence even if there are no aspirations of staying with the dog-show game later in life. Frequently, Junior Showmanship becomes the background of those who become successful exhibitors/handlers in the future. In some instances it is taken very seriously, and success is measured in terms of wins. The Junior Handler is judged solely on his ability and skill in presenting his dog. The dog's conformation is not to be considered by the judge. Even so the condition and grooming of the dog may be a reflection upon the handler.

Usually the matches and point shows include different classes. The Junior Handler's dog may be entered in a breed or obedience class and even shown by another person in that class. Junior Showmanship classes are usually divided by age and perhaps sex. The age is determined by the handler's age on the day of the show.

CANINE GOOD CITIZEN

The AKC sponsors a program to encourage dog owners to train their dogs. Local clubs perform the pass/fail tests, and dogs who pass are awarded a Canine Good Citizen Certificate.

Proof of vaccination is required at the time of participation. The test includes:

1. Accepting a friendly stranger.
2. Sitting politely for petting.
3. Appearance and grooming.
4. Walking on a loose leash.
5. Walking through a crowd.
6. Sit and down on command/staying in place.
7. Come when called.
8. Reaction to another dog.
9. Reactions to distractions.
10. Supervised separation.

If more effort was made by pet owners to accomplish these exercises, fewer dogs would be cast off to the humane shelter.

Sitting still for petting and grooming is one requirement for a canine good citizen. It looks like this Lhasa has passed the test.

OBEDIENCE

Obedience is necessary, without a doubt, but it can also become a wonderful hobby or even an obsession. Obedience classes and competition can provide wonderful companionship, not only with your dog but with your classmates or fellow competitors. It is always gratifying to discuss your dog's problems with others who have had similar experiences. The AKC acknowledged Obedience around 1936, and it has changed tremendously even though many of the exercises are basically the same. Today, obedience competition is just that—very competitive. Even so, it is possible for every obedience exhibitor to come home a winner (by earning qualifying scores) even though he/ she may not earn a placement in the class.

Most of the obedience titles are awarded after earning three qualifying scores (legs) in the appropriate class under three

A champion of champions, this Lhasa Apso wins Best in Show at the 1990 World Dog Show, an international show held in different cities each year.

different judges. These classes offer a perfect score of 200, which is extremely rare. Each of the class exercises has its own point value. A leg is earned after receiving a score of at least 170 and at least 50 percent of the points available in each exercise. The titles are:

Companion Dog—CD
Companion Dog Excellent—CDX
Utility Dog—UD

After achieving the UD title, you may feel inclined to go after the UDX and/or OTCh. The UDX (Utility Dog Excellent) title went into effect in January 1994. It is not easily attained. The title requires qualifying simultaneously ten times in Open B and Utility B but not necessarily at consecutive shows.

The OTCh (Obedience Trial Champion) is awarded after the dog has earned his UD and then goes on to earn 100 championship points, a first place in Utility, a first place in Open and another first place in either class. The placements must be won under three different judges at all-breed obedience trials. The points are determined by the number of dogs competing in the Open B and Utility B classes. The OTCh title precedes the dog's name.

Obedience matches (AKC Sanctioned, Fun, and Show and Go) are usually available. Usually they are sponsored by the local obedience clubs. When preparing an obedience dog for a title, you will find matches very helpful. Fun Matches and Show and Go Matches are more lenient in allowing you to make corrections in the ring. This type of training is usually very necessary for the Open and Utility Classes. AKC Sanctioned Obedience Matches do not allow corrections in the ring since they must abide by the AKC Obedience Regulations. If you are interested in showing in obedience, then you should contact the AKC for a copy of the Obedience Regulations.

TRACKING

Tracking is officially classified obedience. There are three tracking titles available: Tracking Dog (TD), Tracking Dog Excellent (TDX), Variable Surface Tracking (VST). If all three tracking titles are obtained, then the dog officially becomes a CT (Champion Tracker). The CT will go in front of the dog's name.

Lhasas can do anything! Tabu's Special Delivery, ROM shows her swimming skills by taking a dip in the pool.

A TD may be earned anytime and does not have to follow the other obedience titles. There are many exhibitors that prefer tracking to obedience, and there are others who do both.

AGILITY

Agility was first introduced by John Varley in England at the Crufts Dog Show, February 1978, but Peter Meanwell, competitor and judge, actually developed the idea. It was officially recognized in the early '80s. Agility is extremely popular in England and Canada and growing in popularity in the U.S. The AKC acknowledged agility in August 1994. Dogs must be at least 12 months of age to be entered. It is a fascinating sport that the dog, handler and spectators enjoy to the

Even if you never enter a show, the training you give your Lhasa Apso can only benefit him in the long run.

utmost. Agility is a spectator sport! The dog performs off lead. The handler either runs with his dog or positions himself on the course and directs his dog with verbal and hand signals over a timed course over or through a variety of obstacles including a time out or pause. One of the main drawbacks to agility is finding a place to train. The obstacles take up a lot of space and it is very time consuming to put up and take down courses.

The titles earned at AKC agility trials are Novice Agility Dog (NAD), Open Agility Dog (OAD), Agility Dog Excellent (ADX), and Master Agility Excellent (MAX). In order to acquire an agility title, a dog must earn a qualifying score in its respective class on three separate occasions under two different judges. The MAX will be awarded after earning ten qualifying scores in the Agility Excellent Class.

PERFORMANCE TESTS

During the last decade the American Kennel Club has promoted performance tests—those events that test the different breeds' natural abilities. This type of event encourages a handler to devote even more time to his dog and retain the natural instincts of his breed heritage. It is an important part of the wonderful world of dogs.

GENERAL INFORMATION

Obedience, tracking and agility allow the purebred dog with an Indefinite Listing Privilege (ILP) number or a limited registration to be exhibited and earn titles. Application must be made to the AKC for an ILP number.

The American Kennel Club publishes a monthly *Events* magazine that is part of the *Gazette*, their official journal for the sport of purebred dogs. The *Events* section lists upcoming shows and the secretary or superintendent for them. The majority of the conformation shows in the U.S. are overseen by licensed superintendents. Generally the entry closing date is approximately two-and-a-half weeks before the actual show. Point shows are fairly expensive, while the match shows cost about one third of the point show entry fee. Match shows

The Lhasa Apso is a versatile and intelligent dog that can excel in many activities.

usually take entries the day of the show but some are pre-entry. The best way to find match show information is through your local kennel club. Upon asking, the AKC can provide you with a list of superintendents, and you can write and ask to be put on their mailing lists.

Obedience trial and tracking test information is available through the AKC. Frequently these events are not superintended, but put on by the host club. Therefore you would make the entry with the event's secretary.

As you have read, there are numerous activities you can share with your dog. Regardless what you do, it does take teamwork. Your dog can only benefit from your attention and training. We hope this chapter has enlightened you and hope, if nothing else, you will attend a show here and there. Perhaps you will start with a puppy kindergarten class, and who knows where it may lead!

Training to compete is not an easy task, but the satisfaction you'll receive when you accomplish your goals is rewarding for both you and your Lhasa.

HEALTH CARE

Veterinary medicine has become far more sophisticated than what was available to our ancestors. This can be attributed to the increase in household pets and consequently the demand for better care for them. Also human medicine has become far more complex. Today diagnostic testing in veterinary medicine parallels human diagnostics. Because of better technology we can expect our pets to live healthier lives thereby increasing their life spans.

THE FIRST CHECK UP

You will want to take your new puppy/dog in for its first check up within 48 to 72 hours after acquiring it. Many breeders strongly recommend this check up and so do the humane shelters. A puppy/dog can appear healthy but it may have a serious problem that is not apparent to the layman. Most pets have some type of a minor flaw that may never cause a real problem.

Maternal antibodies protect puppies against diseases for the first few weeks of life, but vaccinations are needed because the antibodies are only temporarily effective.

Unfortunately if he/she should have a serious problem, you will want to consider the consequences of keeping the pet and the attachments that will be formed, which may be broken prematurely. Keep in mind there are many healthy dogs looking for good homes.

This first check up is a good time to establish yourself with the veterinarian and learn the office policy regarding their hours and how they handle emergencies. Usually the breeder or another conscientious pet owner is a good reference for

A puppy is very vulnerable and needs to see a veterinarian within 48 hours of his arrival in his new home.

locating a capable veterinarian. You should be aware that not all veterinarians give the same quality of service. Please do not make your selection on the least expensive clinic, as they may be short changing your pet. There is the possibility that eventually it will cost you more due to improper diagnosis, treatment, etc. If you are selecting a new veterinarian, feel free to ask for a tour of the clinic. You should inquire about making an appointment for a tour since all clinics are working clinics, and therefore may not be available all day for sightseers. You may worry less if you see where your pet will be spending the day if he ever needs to be hospitalized.

THE PHYSICAL EXAM

Your veterinarian will check your pet's overall condition, which includes listening to the heart; checking the respiration; feeling the abdomen, muscles and joints; checking the mouth, which includes the gum color and signs of gum disease along with plaque buildup; checking the ears for signs of an infection or ear mites; examining the eyes; and, last but not least, checking the condition of the skin and coat.

He should ask you questions regarding your pet's eating and elimination habits and invite you to relay your questions. It is a good idea to prepare a list so as not to forget anything. He should discuss the proper diet and the quantity to be fed. If this should differ from your breeder's recommendation, then you should convey to him the breeder's choice and see if he approves. If he recommends changing the diet, then this should be done over a few days so as not to cause a gastrointestinal upset. It is customary to take in a fresh stool sample (just a small amount) for a test for intestinal parasites. It must be fresh, preferably within 12 hours, since the eggs hatch quickly and after hatching will not be observed under the microscope. If your pet isn't obliging then, usually the technician can take one in the clinic.

IMMUNIZATIONS

It is important that you take your puppy/dog's vaccination record with you on your first visit. In case of a puppy, presumably the breeder has seen to the vaccinations up to the time you acquired custody. Veterinarians differ in their vaccination protocol. It is not unusual for your puppy to have received vaccinations for distemper, hepatitis, leptospirosis,

The POPpup™ by Nylabone® is a healthy treat for your Lhasa Apso. Fortified with calcium, it becomes a rich cracker when microwaved.

parvovirus and parainfluenza every two to three weeks from the age of five or six weeks. Usually this is a combined injection and is typically called the DHLPP. The DHLPP is given through at least 12 to 14 weeks of age, and it is customary to continue with another parvovirus vaccine at 16 to 18 weeks. You may wonder why so many immunizations are necessary. No one knows for sure when the puppy's maternal antibodies are gone, although it is customarily accepted that distemper antibodies are gone by 12 weeks. Usually parvovirus antibodies are gone by 16 to 18 weeks of age. However, it is possible for the maternal antibodies to be gone at a

Your veterinarian should put your Lhasa Apso on an immunization schedule to protect him from certain diseases.

Dogs can pick up diseases from other dogs, so make sure your Lhasa has his proper vaccinations before taking him out to make friends.

Your Lhasa should receive all his immunizations and proper health care early in life. His first birthday party should be a happy healthy one!

much earlier age or even a later age. Therefore immunizations are started at an early age. The vaccine will not give immunity as long as there are maternal antibodies.

The rabies vaccination is given at three or six months of age depending on your local laws. A vaccine for bordetella (kennel cough) is advisable and can be given anytime from the age of five weeks. The coronavirus is not commonly given unless there is a problem locally. The Lyme vaccine is necessary in endemic areas. Lyme disease has been reported in 47 states.

Distemper

This is virtually an incurable disease. If the dog recovers, he is subject to severe nervous disorders. The virus attacks every tissue in the body and resembles a bad cold with a fever. It can cause a runny nose and eyes and cause gastrointestinal disorders, including a poor appetite, vomiting and diarrhea. The virus is carried by raccoons, foxes, wolves, mink and other dogs. Unvaccinated youngsters and senior citizens are very susceptible. This is still a common disease.

Your Lhasa will need regular checkups to maintain his good health and prevent potential problems.

Hepatitis

This is a virus that is most serious in very young dogs. It is spread by contact with an infected animal or its stool or urine. The virus affects the liver and kidneys and is characterized by high fever, depression and lack of appetite. Recovered animals may be afflicted with chronic illnesses.

Leptospirosis

This is a bacterial disease transmitted by contact with the urine of an infected dog, rat or other wildlife. It produces severe symptoms of fever, depression, jaundice and internal bleeding and was fatal before the vaccine was developed. Recovered dogs can be carriers, and the disease can be transmitted from dogs to humans.

Parvovirus

This was first noted in the late 1970s and is still a fatal disease. However, with proper vaccinations, early diagnosis and prompt treatment, it is a manageable disease. It attacks the bone marrow and intestinal tract. The symptoms include depression, loss of appetite, vomiting, diarrhea and collapse. Immediate medical attention is of the essence.

Rabies

This is shed in the saliva and is carried by raccoons, skunks, foxes, other dogs and cats. It attacks nerve tissue, resulting in paralysis and death. Rabies can be transmitted to people and is virtually always fatal. This disease is reappearing in the suburbs.

Bordetella (Kennel Cough)

The symptoms are coughing, sneezing, hacking and retching accompanied by nasal discharge usually lasting from a few days to several weeks. There are several disease-producing organisms responsible for this disease. The present vaccines are helpful but do not protect for all the strains. It usually is not life threatening but in some instances it can progress to a serious bronchopneumonia. The disease is highly contagious. The vaccination should be given routinely for dogs that come in contact with other dogs, such as through boarding, training class or visits to the groomer.

Coronavirus

This is usually self limiting and not life threatening. It was first noted in the late '70s about a year before parvovirus. The virus produces a yellow/brown stool and there may be depression, vomiting and diarrhea.

Lyme Disease

This was first diagnosed in the United States in 1976 in Lyme, CT in people who lived in close proximity to the deer

Bordetella attached to canine cilia. Otherwise known as kennel cough, this highly contagious disease should be vaccinated against routinely.

tick. Symptoms may include acute lameness, fever, swelling of joints and loss of appetite. Your veterinarian can advise you if you live in an endemic area.

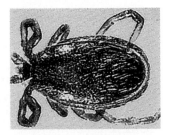

After your puppy has completed his puppy vaccinations, you will continue to booster the DHLPP once a year. It is customary to booster the rabies one year after the first vaccine and then, depending on where you live, it should be boostered every year or every three years. This depends on your local laws. The Lyme and corona vaccines are boostered annually and it is recommended that the bordetella be boostered every six to eight months.

The deer tick is the most common carrier of Lyme disease. Photo courtesy of Virbac Laboratories, Inc., Fort Worth, Texas.

ANNUAL VISIT

I would like to impress the importance of the annual check up, which would include the booster vaccinations, check for intestinal parasites and test for heartworm. Today in our very busy world it is rush, rush and see "how much you can get for how little." Unbelievably, some non-veterinary businesses have entered into the vaccination business. More harm than good can come to your dog through improper vaccinations, possibly from inferior vaccines and/or the wrong schedule. More than likely you truly care about your companion dog and over the years you have devoted much time and expense to his well being. Perhaps you are unaware that a vaccination is not just a vaccination. There is more involved. Please, please follow through with regular physical examinations. It is so important for your veterinarian to know your dog and this is especially true during middle age through the geriatric years. More than likely your older dog will require more than one physical a year. The annual physical is good preventive medicine. Through early diagnosis and subsequent treatment your dog can maintain a longer and better quality of life.

INTESTINAL PARASITES

Hookworms

These are almost microscopic intestinal worms that can cause anemia and therefore serious problems, including death, in young puppies. Hookworms can be transmitted to humans through penetration of the skin. Puppies may be born with them.

Roundworms

These are spaghetti-like worms that can cause a potbellied appearance and dull coat along with more severe symptoms, such as vomiting, diarrhea and coughing. Puppies acquire these while in the mother's uterus and through lactation. Both hookworms and roundworms may be acquired through ingestion.

Whipworms

These have a three-month life cycle and are not acquired through the dam. They cause intermittent diarrhea usually with mucus. Whipworms are possibly the most difficult worm to

Hookworms are almost microscopic intestinal worms that can cause anemia and therefore serious problems, even death.

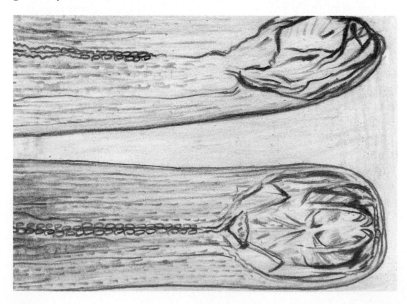

eradicate. Their eggs are very resistant to most environmental factors and can last for years until the proper conditions enable them to mature. Whipworms are seldom seen in the stool.

Intestinal parasites are more prevalent in some areas than others. Climate, soil and contamination are big factors contributing to the incidence of intestinal parasites. Eggs are passed in the stool, lay on the ground and then become infective in a certain number of days. Each of the above worms has a different life cycle. Your best chance of becoming and remaining worm-free is to always pooper-scoop your yard. A fenced-in yard keeps stray dogs out, which is certainly helpful.

I would recommend having a fecal examination on your dog twice a year or more often if there is a problem. If your dog has a positive fecal sample, then he will be given the appropriate medication and you will be asked to bring back another stool sample in a certain period of time (depending on the type of worm) and then be rewormed. This process goes on until he

Roundworm eggs, as seen on a fecal evaluation. The eggs must develop for at least 12 days before they are infective.

has at least two negative samples. The different types of worms require different medications. You will be wasting your money and doing your dog an injustice by buying over-the-counter medication without first consulting your veterinarian.

OTHER INTERNAL PARASITES

Coccidiosis and Giardiasis

These protozoal infections usually affect puppies, especially in places where large numbers of puppies are brought together. Older dogs may harbor these infections but do not show signs unless they are stressed. Symptoms include diarrhea, weight loss and lack of appetite. These infections are not always apparent in the fecal examination.

Tapeworms

Seldom apparent on fecal floatation, they are diagnosed frequently as rice-like segments around the dog's anus and the base of the tail. Tapeworms are long, flat and ribbon like, sometimes several feet in length, and made up of many segments about five-eighths of an inch long. The two most common types of tapeworms found in the dog are:

(1) First the larval form of the flea tapeworm parasite must mature in an intermediate host, the flea, before it can become infective. Your dog acquires this by ingesting the flea through licking and chewing.

(2) Rabbits, rodents and certain large game animals serve as intermediate hosts for other species of tapeworms. If your dog should eat one of these infected hosts, then he can acquire tapeworms.

HEARTWORM DISEASE

This is a worm that resides in the heart and adjacent blood vessels of the lung that produces microfilaria, which circulate in the bloodstream. It is possible for a dog to be infected with any number of worms from one to a hundred that can be 6 to 14 inches long. It is a life-threatening disease, expensive to treat and easily prevented. Depending on where you live, your veterinarian may recommend a preventive year-round and either an annual or semiannual blood test. The most common preventive is given once a month.

EXTERNAL PARASITES

Fleas

These pests are not only the dog's worst enemy but also enemy to the owner's pocketbook. Preventing is less expensive than treating, but regardless we'd prefer to spend our money elsewhere.

Dirofilia—adult worms in a heart of a dog. Courtesy of Merck Ag Vet.

Your Lhasa can pick up parasites like fleas and ticks when outside. Make sure you check your dog's coat thoroughly after playing outdoors.

Likely, the majority of our dogs are allergic to the bite of a flea, and in many cases it only takes one flea bite. The protein in the flea's saliva is the culprit. Allergic dogs have a reaction, which usually results in a "hot spot." More than likely such a reaction will involve a trip to the veterinarian for treatment. Yes, prevention is less expensive. Fortunately today there are several good products available.

If there is a flea infestation, no one product is going to correct the problem. Not only will the dog require treatment so will the environment. In general flea collars are not very effective although there is now available an "egg" collar that will kill the eggs on the dog. Dips are the most economical but they are messy. There are some effective shampoos and treatments available through pet shops and veterinarians. An oral tablet arrived on the American market in 1995 and was popular in Europe the previous year. It sterilizes the female flea but will not kill adult fleas. Therefore the tablet, which is given monthly, will decrease the flea population but is not a "cure-all." Those dogs that suffer from flea-bite allergy will still be subjected to the bite of the flea. Another popular parasiticide is permethrin, which is applied to the back of the dog in one or two places depending on the dog's weight. This product works as a repellent causing the flea to get "hot feet" and jump off. Do not confuse this product with some of the organophosphates that are also applied to the dog's back.

Some products are not usable on young puppies. Treating fleas should be done under your veterinarian's guidance. Frequently it is necessary to combine products and the layman does not have the knowledge regarding possible toxicities. It is hard to believe but there are a few dogs that do have a natural resistance to fleas. Nevertheless it would be wise to treat all pets at the same time. Don't forget your cats. Cats just love to prowl the neighborhood and consequently return with unwanted guests. Check with your veterinarian.

Adult fleas live on the dog but their eggs drop off the dog into the environment. There they go through four larval stages before reaching adulthood, and thereby are able to jump back on the poor unsuspecting dog. The cycle resumes and takes between 21 to 28 days under ideal conditions. There are environmental products available that will kill both the adult fleas and the larvae.

Ticks

Ticks carry Rocky Mountain Spotted Fever, Lyme disease and can cause tick paralysis. They should be removed with tweezers, trying to pull out the head. The jaws carry disease. There is a tick preventive collar that does an excellent job. The ticks automatically back out on those dogs wearing collars.

Sarcoptic Mange

This is a mite that is difficult to find on skin scrapings. The pinnal reflex is a good indicator of this disease. Rub the ends of the pinna (ear) together and the dog will start scratching with his foot. Sarcoptes are highly contagious to other dogs and to humans although they do not live long on humans. They cause intense itching.

Demodectic Mange

This is a mite that is passed from the dam to her puppies. It affects youngsters age three to ten months. Diagnosis is confirmed by skin scraping. Small areas of alopecia around the eyes, lips and/or forelegs become visible. There is little itching unless there is a secondary bacterial infection. Some breeds are afflicted more than others.

Cheyletiella

This causes intense itching and is diagnosed by skin scraping. It lives in the outer layers of the skin of dogs, cats, rabbits and humans. Yellow-gray scales may be found on the back and the rump, top of the head and the nose.

A regular careful grooming regimen is the best way to control any external parasites on your Lhasa Apso.

TO BREED OR NOT TO BREED

More than likely your breeder has requested that you have your puppy neutered or spayed. Your breeder's request is based on what is healthiest for your dog and what is most

beneficial for your breed. Experienced and conscientious breeders devote many years into developing a bloodline. In order to do this, he makes every effort to plan each breeding in regard to conformation, temperament and health. This type of breeder does his best to perform the necessary testing (i.e., OFA, CERF, testing for inherited blood disorders, thyroid, etc.). Testing is expensive and sometimes very disheartening when a favorite dog doesn't pass his health tests. The health history pertains not only to the breeding stock but to the immediate ancestors. Reputable breeders do not want their offspring to be bred indiscriminately. Therefore you

Spaying or neutering your pet Lhasa will help prevent certain diseases as well as help control the pet population.

may be asked to neuter or spay your puppy. Of course there is always the exception, and your breeder may agree to let you breed your dog under his direct supervision. This is an important concept. More and more effort is being made to breed healthier dogs.

Spay/Neuter

There are numerous benefits of performing this surgery at six months of age. Unspayed females are subject to mammary and ovarian cancer. In order to prevent mammary cancer she must be spayed prior to her first heat cycle. Later in life, an unspayed female may develop a pyometra (an infected uterus), which is definitely life threatening.

Spaying is performed under a general anesthetic and is easy on the young dog. As you might expect it is a little harder on

the older dog, but that is no reason to deny

Your Lhasa should have a strong easy gait. Any irregularities in your dog's stride should be reported to your veterinarian.

her the surgery. The surgery removes the ovaries and uterus. It is important to remove all the ovarian tissue. If some is left behind, she could remain attractive to males. In order to view the ovaries, a reasonably long incision is necessary. An ovariohysterectomy is considered major surgery.

Neutering the male at a young age will inhibit some characteristic male behavior that owners frown upon. Some boys will not hike their legs and mark territory if they are neutered at six months of age. Also neutering at a young age has hormonal benefits, lessening the chance of hormonal aggressiveness.

Surgery involves removing the testicles but leaving the scrotum. If there should be a retained testicle, then he definitely needs to be neutered before the age of two or three years. Retained testicles can develop into cancer. Unneutered males are at risk for testicular cancer, perineal fistulas, perianal tumors and fistulas and prostatic disease.

Intact males and females are prone to housebreaking accidents. Females urinate frequently before, during and after heat cycles, and males tend to mark territory if there is a female in heat. Males may show the *Reputable breeders will screen all Lhasa Apsos before using them in their breeding programs.*

You must be careful to check that your Lhasa's eyes are clear and free of any signs of irritation.

same behavior if there is a visiting dog or guests.

Surgery involves a sterile operating procedure equivalent to human surgery. The incision site is shaved, surgically scrubbed and draped. The veterinarian wears a sterile surgical gown, cap, mask and gloves. Anesthesia should be monitored by a registered technician. It is customary for the veterinarian to recommend a pre-anesthetic blood screening, looking for metabolic problems and a ECG rhythm strip to check for normal heart function. Today anesthetics are equal to human anesthetics, which enables your dog to walk out of the clinic the same day as surgery.

Some folks worry about their dog gaining weight after being neutered or spayed. This is usually not the case. It is true that some dogs may be less active so they could develop a problem, but most dogs are just as active as they were before surgery. However, if your dog should begin to gain, then you need to decrease his food and see to it that he gets a little more exercise.

DENTAL CARE for Your Dog's Life

S o you've got a new puppy! You also have a new set of puppy teeth in your household. Anyone who has ever raised a puppy is abundantly aware of these new teeth. Your puppy will chew anything it can reach, chase your shoelaces, and play "tear the rag" with any piece of clothing it can find. When puppies are newly born, they have no teeth. At about four weeks of age, puppies of most breeds begin to develop their deciduous or baby teeth. They begin eating semi-solid food, fighting and biting with their litter mates, and learning discipline from their mother. As their new teeth come in, they inflict more pain on their mother's breasts, so her feeding sessions become less frequent and shorter. By six or eight weeks, the mother will start growling to warn her pups when they are fighting too roughly or hurting her as they nurse too much with their new teeth.

Your grooming routine should include cleaning your Lhasa's teeth and examining his mouth.

Puppies need to chew. It is a necessary part of their physical and mental development. They develop muscles and necessary life skills as they drag objects around, fight over possession, and vocalize alerts and warnings. Puppies chew on things to explore their world. They are using their sense of taste to determine what is food and what is not. How else can they tell an electrical cord from a lizard? At about four months of age, most puppies begin shedding their baby teeth. Often these teeth need some help

A Nylafloss™ made of nylon can literally floss your Lhasa's teeth while he plays.

to come out and make way for the permanent teeth. The incisors (front teeth) will be replaced first. Then, the adult canine or fang teeth erupt. When the baby tooth is not shed before the permanent tooth comes in, veterinarians call it a retained deciduous tooth. This condition will often cause gum infections by trapping hair and debris between the permanent tooth and the retained baby tooth. Nylafloss® is an excellent device for puppies to use. They can toss it, drag it, and chew on the many surfaces it presents. The baby teeth can catch in the nylon material, aiding in their removal. Puppies that have adequate chew toys will have less destructive behavior, develop more physically, and have less chance of retained deciduous teeth.

During the first year, your dog should be seen by your veterinarian at regular intervals. Your veterinarian will let you know when to bring in your puppy for vaccinations and parasite examinations. At each visit, your veterinarian should inspect the lips, teeth, and mouth as part of a complete physical examination. You should take some part in the maintenance of your dog's oral health. You should examine your dog's mouth weekly throughout his first year to make sure there are no sores, foreign objects, tooth problems, etc. If your

The Hercules™ is made of very tough polyurethane. The raised dental tips massage the gums and mechanically remove the plaque that they encounter during the chewing process.

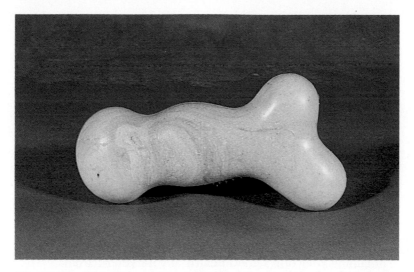

The Galileo™ is flavored to appeal to your Lhasa and annealed so it has a relatively soft outer layer. It is a necessary chew device and Lhasa pacifier. dog drools excessively, shakes its head, or has bad breath, consult your veterinarian. By the time your dog is six months old, the permanent teeth are all in and plaque can start to accumulate on the tooth surfaces. This is when your dog needs to develop good dental-care habits to prevent calculus build-up on its teeth. Brushing is best. That is a fact that cannot be denied. However, some dogs do not like their teeth brushed regularly, or you may not be able to accomplish the task. In that case, you should consider a product that will help prevent plaque and calculus build-up.

The Plaque Attackers® and Galileo Bone® are other excellent choices for the first three years of a dog's life. Their shapes make them interesting for the dog. As the dog chews on them, the solid polyurethane massages the gums which improves the blood circulation to the periodontal tissues. Projections on the chew devices increase the surface and are in contact with the tooth for more efficient cleaning. The unique shape and consistency prevent your dog from exerting excessive force on his own teeth or from breaking off pieces of the bone. If your dog is an aggressive chewer or weighs more than 55 pounds (25 kg), you should consider giving him a Nylabone®, the most durable chew product on the market.

The Gumabones®, made by the Nylabone Company, is constructed of strong polyurethane, which is softer than nylon. Less powerful chewers prefer the Gumabones® to the Nylabones®. A super option for your dog is the Hercules Bone®, a uniquely shaped bone named after the great Olympian for its exception strength. Like all Nylabone products, they are specially scented to make them attractive to your dog. Ask your veterinarian about these bones and he will validate the good doctor's prescription: Nylabones® not only give your dog a good chewing workout but also help to save your dog's teeth (and even his life, as it protects him from possible fatal periodontal diseases).

By the time dogs are four years old, 75% of them have periodontal disease. It is the most common infection in dogs. Yearly examinations by your veterinarian are essential to maintaining your dog's good health. If your veterinarian detects periodontal disease, he or she may recommend a prophylactic cleaning. To do a thorough cleaning, it will be necessary to put your dog under anesthesia. With modern gas anesthetics and monitoring equipment, the procedure is pretty safe. Your veterinarian will scale the teeth with an ultrasound scaler or hand instrument. This removes the calculus from the teeth. If there are calculus deposits below the gum line, the veterinarian will plane the roots to make them smooth. After all of the calculus has been removed, the teeth are polished with pumice in a polishing cup. If any medical or surgical treatment is needed, it is done at this time. The final step would be fluoride treatment and your follow-up treatment at

Raised dental tips help to combat plaque and tartar on the surface of every Plaque Attacker™ bone. Safe for aggressive chewers and ruggedly constructed to last, these bones provide your dog with hours of enjoyment.

home. If the periodontal disease is advanced, the veterinarian may prescribe a medicated mouth rinse or antibiotics for use at home. Make sure your dog has safe, clean and attractive chew toys and treats. Chooz® treats are another way of using a consumable treat to help keep your dog's teeth clean.

Provide your Lhasa Apso with plenty of Nylabones® to keep his teeth healthy and occupied.

2-Brush™ by Nylabone® is made with two toothbrushes to clean both sides of your dog's teeth at the same time. Each brush contains a reservoir designed to apply the toothpaste, which is specially formulated for dogs, directly into the toothbrush.

Rawhide is the most popular of all materials for a dog to chew. This has never been good

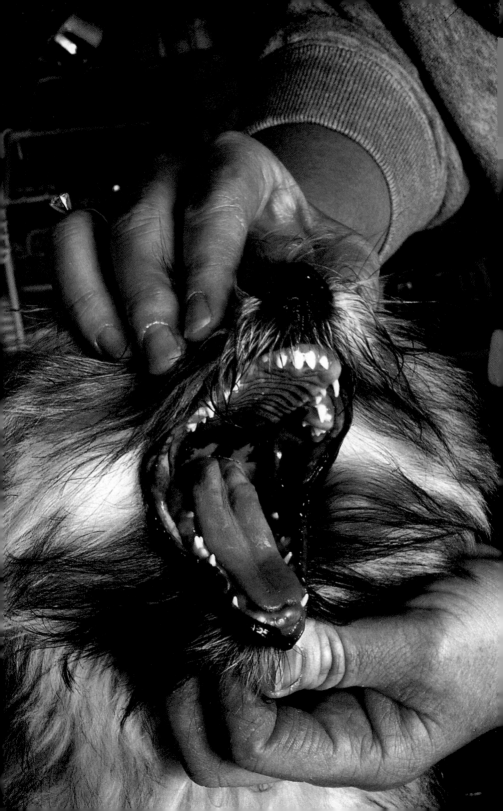

news to dog owners, because rawhide is inherently very dangerous for dogs. Thousands of dogs have died from rawhide, having swallowed the hide after it has become soft and mushy, only to cause stomach and intestinal blockage. A new rawhide product on the market has finally solved the problem of rawhide: molded Roar-Hide® from Nylabone. These are composed of processed, cut up, and melted American rawhide injected into your dog's favorite shape: a dog bone. These dog-safe devices smell and taste like rawhide but don't break up. The ridges on the bones help to fight tartar build-up on the teeth and they last ten times longer than the usual rawhide chews.

If you train your Lhasa to have good chewing habits as a puppy, he will have healthier teeth throughout his life.

As your dog ages, professional examination and cleaning should become more frequent. The mouth should be inspected at least once a year. Your veterinarian may recommend visits every six months. In the geriatric patient, organs such as the heart, liver, and kidneys do not function as well as when they were young. Your veterinarian will probably want to test these organs' functions prior to using general anesthesia for dental cleaning. If your dog is a good chewer and you work closely with your veterinarian, your dog can keep all of its teeth all of its life. However, as your dog ages, his sense of smell, sight, and taste will diminish. He may not have the desire to chase, trap or chew his toys. He will also not have the energy to chew for long periods, as arthritis and periodontal disease make chewing painful. This will leave you with more responsibility for keeping his teeth clean and healthy. The dog that would not let you brush his teeth at one year of age, may let you brush his teeth now that he is ten years old.

A thorough oral examination should be a part of your Lhasa's regular veterinary checkup.

If you train your dog with good chewing habits as a puppy, he will have healthier teeth throughout his life.

TRAVELING with Your Dog

The earlier you start traveling with your new puppy or dog, the better. He needs to become accustomed to traveling. However, some dogs are nervous riders and become carsick easily. It is helpful if he starts with an empty stomach. Do not despair, as it will go better if you continue taking him with you on short fun rides. How would you feel if every time you rode in the car you stopped at the doctor's for an injection? You would soon dread that nasty car. Older dogs that tend to get carsick may have more of a problem adjusting to traveling. Those dogs that are having a serious problem may benefit from some medication prescribed by the veterinarian.

You'll never have to leave your Lhasa behind if you accustom him to traveling at an early age.

Do give your dog a chance to relieve himself before getting into the car. It is a good idea to be prepared for a clean up with a leash, paper towels, bag and terry cloth towel.

The safest place for your dog is in a fiberglass crate, although close confinement can promote carsickness in some dogs. If your dog is nervous you can try letting him ride on the seat next to you or in someone's lap.

An alternative to the crate would be to use a car harness made for dogs and/or a safety strap attached to the harness or collar. Whatever you do, do not let your dog ride in the back of a pickup truck unless he is securely tied on a very short lead. I've seen trucks stop quickly and, even though the dog was tied, it fell out and was dragged.

Another advantage of the crate is that it is a safe place to leave him if you need to run into the store. Otherwise you wouldn't be able to leave the windows down. Keep in mind that while many dogs are overly protective in their crates, this

Crates are the safest way for your Lhasa Apso to travel in the car.

may not be enough to deter dognappers. In some states it is against the law to leave a dog in the car unattended.

Never leave a dog loose in the car wearing a collar and leash. More than one dog has killed himself by hanging. Do not let him put his head out an open window. Foreign debris can be blown into his eyes. When leaving your dog unattended in a car, consider the temperature. It can take less than five minutes to reach temperatures over 100 degrees Fahrenheit.

TRIPS

Perhaps you are taking a trip. Give consideration to what is best for your dog–traveling with you or boarding. When

Lhasas are such easygoing and adaptable dogs, they can accompany you anywhere! traveling by car, van or motor home, you need to think ahead about locking your vehicle. In all probability you have many valuables in the car and do not wish to leave it unlocked. Perhaps most valuable and not replaceable is your dog. Give thought to securing your vehicle and providing adequate ventilation for him. Another consideration for you when traveling with your dog is medical problems that may arise and little inconveniences, such as exposure to external parasites. Some areas of the country are quite flea infested. You may want to carry flea spray with you. This is even a good idea when staying in motels. Quite possibly you are not the only occupant of the room.

Unbelievably many motels and even hotels do allow canine guests, even some very first-class ones. Gaines Pet Foods

Corporation publishes *Touring With Towser*, a directory of domestic hotels and motels that accommodate guests with dogs. Their address is Gaines TWT, PO Box 5700, Kankakee, IL, 60902. Call ahead to any motel that you may be considering and see if they accept pets. Sometimes it is necessary to pay a deposit against room damage. The management may feel reassured if you mention that your dog will be crated. If you do travel with your dog, take along plenty of baggies so that you can clean up after him. When we all do our share in cleaning up, we make it possible for motels to continue accepting our pets. As a matter of fact, you should practice cleaning up everywhere you take your dog.

The well-trained and well-socialized Lhasa Apso makes a suitable traveling companion for anyone.

Depending on where your are traveling, you may need an up-to-date health certificate issued by your veterinarian. It is good policy to take along your dog's medical information, which would include the name, address and phone number of your veterinarian, vaccination record, rabies certificate, and any medication he is taking.

AIR TRAVEL

When traveling by air, you need to contact the airlines to check their policy. Usually you have to make arrangements up to a couple of weeks in advance for traveling with your dog. The airlines require your dog to travel in an airline approved fiberglass crate. Usually these can be purchased through the airlines but they are also readily available in most pet-supply stores. If your dog is not accustomed to a crate, then it is a good idea to get him acclimated to it before your trip. The day of the actual trip you should withhold water about one hour ahead of departure and no food for about 12 hours. The airlines generally have temperature restrictions, which do not allow pets to travel if it is either too cold or too hot. Frequently these restrictions are based on the temperatures at the departure and arrival airports. It's best to inquire about a health certificate. These usually need to be issued within ten days of departure. You should arrange for non-stop, direct flights and if a commuter plane should be involved, check to see if it will carry dogs. Some don't. The Humane Society of the United States has put together a tip sheet for airline traveling. You can receive a copy by sending a self-addressed stamped envelope to:

The Humane Society of the United States
Tip Sheet
2100 L Street NW
Washington, DC 20037.

Regulations differ for traveling outside of the country and are sometimes changed without notice. Well in advance you need to write or call the appropriate consulate or agricultural department for instructions. Some countries have lengthy quarantines (six months), and countries differ in their rabies vaccination requirements. For instance, it may have to be given at least 30 days ahead of your departure.

Do make sure your dog is wearing proper identification including your name, phone number and city. You never know when you might be in an accident and separated from your dog. Or your dog could be frightened and somehow manage to escape and run away.

Another suggestion would be to carry in-case-of-emergency instructions. These would include the address and phone number of a relative or friend, your veterinarian's name, address and phone number, and your dog's medical information.

BOARDING KENNELS

Perhaps you have decided that you need to board your dog. Your veterinarian can recommend a good boarding facility or possibly a pet sitter that will come to your house. It is customary for the boarding kennel to ask for proof of vaccination for the DHLPP, rabies and bordetella vaccine. The bordetella should have been given within six months of boarding. This is for your protection. If they do not ask for this proof I would not board at their kennel. Ask about flea control. Those dogs that suffer flea-bite allergy can get in trouble at a boarding kennel. Unfortunately boarding kennels are limited on how much they are able to do.

For more information on pet sitting, contact NAPPS:
National Association of Professional Pet Sitters
1200 G Street, NW
Suite 760
Washington, DC 20005.

Some pet clinics have technicians that pet sit and technicians that board clinic patients in their homes. This may be an alternative for you. Ask your veterinarian if they have an employee that can help you. There is a definite advantage of having a technician care for your dog, especially if your dog is on medication or is a senior citizen.

You may be able to take your Lhasas with you when you travel if you find accommodations that will accept your dogs. These Lhasa pups look ready to roll!

You can write for a copy of *Traveling With Your Pet* from ASPCA, Education Department, 441 E. 92nd Street, New York, NY 10128.

IDENTIFICATION and Finding the Lost Dog

There are several ways of identifying your dog. The old standby is a collar with dog license, rabies, and ID tags. Unfortunately collars have a way of being separated from the dog and tags fall off. We're not suggesting you shouldn't use a collar and tags. If they stay intact and on the dog, they are the quickest way of identification.

For several years owners have been tattooing their dogs. Some tattoos use a number with a registry. Here lies the problem because there are several registries to check. If you wish to tattoo, use your social security number. The humane shelters have the means to trace it. It is usually done on the inside of the rear thigh. The area is first shaved and numbed. There is no pain, although a few dogs do not like the buzzing sound. Occasionally tattooing is not legible and needs to be redone.

The newest method of identification is microchipping. The microchip is a computer chip that is no larger than a grain of rice. The veterinarian implants it by injection between the shoulder blades. The dog feels no discomfort. If your dog is lost and picked up by the humane society, they can trace you by scanning the microchip, which has its own code. Microchip scanners are friendly to other brands of microchips and their registries. The microchip comes with a dog tag saying the dog

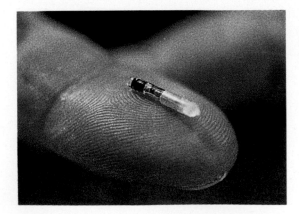

The newest method of identification is microchipping. The microchip is a computer chip no bigger than a grain of rice that can help track your dog's whereabouts.

is microchipped. It is the safest way of identifying your dog.

FINDING THE LOST DOG

I am sure you will agree that there would be little worse than losing your dog. Responsible pet owners rarely lose their dogs. They do not let their dogs run free because they don't want harm to come to them. Not only that but in most, if not all, states there is a leash law.

Be sure to leave your Lhasa in a secure, fenced-in area when unsupervised.

If you cannot be with your Lhasa Apso, confine him to an area of your house to keep him out of trouble.

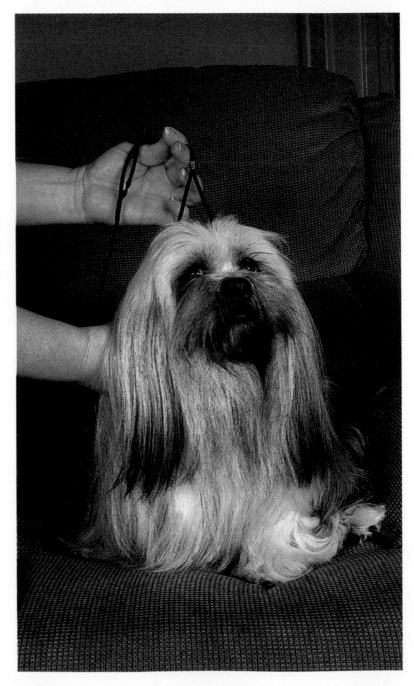

Beware of fenced-in yards. They can be a hazard. Dogs find ways to escape either over or under the fence. Another fast exit is through the gate that perhaps the neighbor's child left unlocked.

Below is a list that hopefully will be of help to you if you need it. Remember don't give up, keep looking. Your dog is worth your efforts.

1. Contact your neighbors and put flyers with a photo on it in their mailboxes. Information you should include would be the dog's name, breed, sex, color, age, source of identification, when your dog was last seen and where, and your name and phone numbers. It may be helpful to say the dog needs medical care. Offer a *reward*.

The persistent Lhasa will never deter from his goal. These Lhasas are determined to get a treat.

2. Check all local shelters daily. It is also possible for your dog to be picked up away from home and end up in an out-of-the-way shelter. Check these too. Go in person. It is not good enough to call. Most shelters are limited on the time they can hold dogs then they are put up for adoption or euthanized. There is the possibility that your dog will not make it to the shelter for several days. Your dog could have been wandering or someone may have tried to keep him.

3. Notify all local veterinarians. Call and send flyers.

4. Call your breeder. Frequently breeders are contacted when one of their breed is found.

5. Contact the rescue group for your breed.

6. Contact local schools—children may have seen your dog.

7. Post flyers at the schools, groceries, gas stations, convenience stores, veterinary clinics, groomers and any other place that will allow them.

Always keep your dog on lead to prevent him from becoming separated from you.

8. Advertise in the newspaper.

9. Advertise on the radio.

BEHAVIOR and Canine Communication

Studies of the human/animal bond point out the importance of the unique relationships that exist between people and their pets. Those of us who share our lives with pets understand the special part they play through companionship, service and protection. For many, the pet/owner bond goes beyond simple companionship; pets are often considered members of the family. A leading pet food manufacturer recently conducted a nationwide survey of pet owners to gauge just how important pets were in their lives. Here's what they found:

The bond between humans and animals, especially loving dogs like Lhasas, is a strong one.

- 76 percent allow their pets to sleep on their beds
- 78 percent think of their pets as their children
- 84 percent display photos of their pets, mostly in their homes
- 84 percent think that their pets react to their own emotions
- 100 percent talk to their pets
- 97 percent think that their pets understand what they're saying

Are you surprised?

Senior citizens show more concern for their own eating habits when they have the responsibility of feeding a dog. Seeing that their dog is routinely exercised encourages the owner to think of schedules that otherwise may seem unimportant to the senior citizen. The older owner may be arthritic and feeling poorly but with responsibility for his dog he has a reason to get up and get moving. It is a big plus if his dog is an attention seeker who will demand such from his owner.

Over the last couple of decades, it has been shown that pets relieve the stress of those who lead busy lives. Owning a pet has been known to lessen the occurrence of heart attack and stroke.

Many single folks thrive on the companionship of a dog. Lifestyles are very different from a long time ago, and today

more individuals seek the single life. However, they receive fulfillment from owning a dog.

Most likely the majority of our dogs live in family environments. The companionship they provide is well worth the effort involved. In my opinion, every child should have the opportunity to have a family dog. Dogs teach responsibility through understanding their care, feelings and even respecting their life cycles. Frequently those children who have not been exposed to dogs grow up afraid of dogs, which isn't good. Dogs sense timidity and some will take advantage of the situation.

The ultimate housedog and companion, the Lhasa Apso enriches the lives of his owners.

Today more dogs are serving as service dogs. Since the origination of the Seeing Eye dogs years ago, we now have trained hearing dogs. Also

dogs are trained to provide service for the handicapped and are able to perform many different tasks for their owners. Search and Rescue dogs, with their handlers, are sent throughout the world to assist in recovery of disaster victims. They are life savers.

Therapy dogs are very popular with nursing homes, and some hospitals even allow them to visit. The inhabitants truly look forward to their visits. They wanted and were allowed to have visiting dogs in their beds to hold and love.

Nationally there is a Pet Awareness Week to educate students and others about the value and basic care of our pets. Many countries take an even greater interest in their pets than Americans do. In those countries the pets are allowed to accompany their owners into restaurants and shops, etc. In the U.S. this freedom is only available to our service dogs. Even so we think very highly of the human/animal bond.

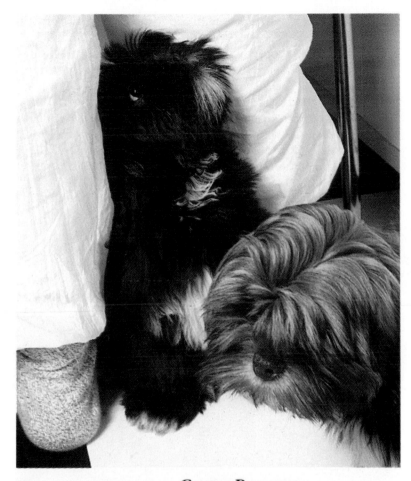

The way your puppy reacts in certain situations can tell you a lot about his personality.

CANINE BEHAVIOR

Canine behavior problems are the number-one reason for pet owners to dispose of their dogs, either through new homes, humane shelters or euthanasia. Unfortunately there are too many owners who are unwilling to devote the necessary time to properly train their dogs. On the other hand, there are those who not only are concerned about inherited health problems but are also aware of the dog's mental stability.

You may realize that a breed and his group relatives (i.e., sporting, hounds, etc.) show tendencies to behavioral characteristics. An experienced breeder can acquaint you with his breed's personality. Unfortunately many breeds are labeled with poor temperaments when actually the breed as a whole is not affected but only a small percentage of individuals within the breed.

Inheritance and environment contribute to the dog's behavior. Some naïve people suggest inbreeding as the cause of bad temperaments. Inbreeding only results in poor behavior if the ancestors carry the trait. If there are excellent temperaments behind the dogs, then inbreeding will promote good temperaments in the offspring. Did you ever consider that inbreeding is what sets the characteristics of a breed? A purebred dog is the end result of inbreeding. This does not spare the mixed-breed dog from the same problems. Mixed-breed dogs frequently are the offspring of purebred dogs.

How can anyone resist an adorable Lhasa puppy? Young Bryce Engen is delighted with the new additions to his household.

Your Lhasa will get along famously with other pets once he is properly socialized. These two friends cozy up on the couch.

Not too many decades ago most of our dogs led a different lifestyle than what is prevalent today. Usually mom stayed home so the dog had human companionship and someone to discipline it if needed. Not much was expected from the dog. Today's mom works and everyone's life is at a much faster pace.

The dog may have to adjust to being a "weekend" dog. The family is gone all day during the week, and the dog is left to his own devices for entertainment. Some dogs sleep all day waiting for their family to come home and others become wigwam wreckers if given the opportunity. Crates do ensure the safety of the dog and the house. However, he could become a physically and emotionally cripple if he doesn't get enough exercise and attention. We still appreciate and want the companionship of our dogs although we expect more from them. In many cases we tend to forget dogs are just that—*dogs* not human beings.

SOCIALIZING AND TRAINING

Many prospective puppy buyers lack experience regarding the proper socialization and training needed to develop the type of pet we all desire. In the first 18 months, training does

143

take some work. It is easier to start proper training before there is a problem that needs to be corrected.

The initial work begins with the breeder. The breeder should start socializing the puppy at five to six weeks of age and cannot let up. Human socializing is critical up through 12 weeks of age and likewise important during the following months. The litter should be left together during the first few weeks but it is necessary to separate them by ten weeks of age. Leaving them together after that time will increase competition for litter dominance. If puppies are not socialized with people by 12 weeks of age, they will be timid in later life.

The eight- to ten-week age period is a fearful time for puppies. They need to be handled very gently around children and adults. There should be no harsh discipline during this time. Starting at 14 weeks of age, the puppy begins the juvenile period, which ends when he reaches sexual maturity around six to 14 months of age. During the juvenile period he needs to be introduced to strangers (adults, children and other dogs) on the home property. At sexual maturity he will begin to bark at strangers and become more protective. Males start to lift their legs to urinate but if you desire you can inhibit this behavior by walking your boy on leash away from trees, shrubs, fences, etc.

Perhaps you are thinking about an older puppy. You need to inquire about the puppy's social experience. If he has lived in a kennel, he may have a hard time adjusting to people and environmental stimuli. Assuming he has had a good social upbringing, there are advantages to an older puppy.

Training includes puppy kindergarten and a minimum of one to two basic training classes. During these classes you will learn how to dominate your

A basket full of love and surprises await every new Lhasa Apso owner.

The busy life of a show dog! Ch. Anbara-Rimar Mary Puppins, CGC takes a break in her hotel room after competing in a national specialty.

youngster. This is especially important if you own a large breed of dog. It is somewhat harder, if not nearly impossible, for some owners to be the Alpha figure when their dog towers over them. You will be taught how to properly restrain your dog. This concept is important. Again it puts you in the Alpha position. All dogs need to be restrained many times during their lives. Believe it or not, some of our worst offenders are the eight-week-old puppies that are brought to our clinic. They need to be gently restrained for a nail trim but the way they carry on you would think we were killing them. In comparison, their vaccination is a "piece of cake." When we ask dogs to do something that is not agreeable to them, then their worst comes out. Life will be easier for your dog if you expose him at a young age to the necessities of life—proper behavior and restraint.

UNDERSTANDING THE DOG'S LANGUAGE

Most authorities agree that the dog is a descendent of the wolf. The dog and wolf have similar traits. For instance both are pack oriented and prefer not to be isolated for long periods of time. Another characteristic is that the dog, like the wolf, looks to the leader–Alpha–for direction. Both the wolf and the dog communicate through body language, not only within their pack but with outsiders.

Every pack has an Alpha figure. The dog looks to you, or should look to you, to be that leader. If your dog doesn't receive the proper training and guidance, he very well may replace you as Alpha. This would be a serious problem and is certainly a disservice to your dog.

Eye contact is one way the Alpha wolf keeps order within his pack. You are Alpha so you must establish eye contact with your puppy. Obviously your puppy will have to look at you. Practice eye contact even if you need to hold his head for five to ten seconds at a time. You can give him a treat as a reward. Make sure your eye contact is gentle and not threatening. Later, if he has been naughty, it is permissible to give him a long, penetrating look. There are some older dogs that never learned eye contact as puppies and cannot accept eye contact. You should avoid eye contact with these dogs since they feel threatened and will retaliate as such.

BODY LANGUAGE

The play bow, when the forequarters are down and the hindquarters are elevated, is an invitation to play. Puppies play fight, which helps them learn the acceptable limits of biting. This is necessary for later in their lives. Nevertheless, an owner may be falsely reassured by the playful nature of his dog's

Rolling over on to his back, this puppy shows his submissive side to his owner—and gets a belly rub as a reward!

aggression. Playful aggression toward another dog or human may be an indication of serious aggression in the future. Owners should never play fight or play tug-of-war with any dog that is inclined to be dominant. Signs of submission are:

1. Avoids eye contact.
2. Active submission—the dog crouches down, ears back and the tail is lowered.
3. Passive submission—the dog rolls on his side with his hindlegs in the air and frequently urinates.

A reluctance to give up his toys may become a dominance problem. Make sure your Lhasa will part with his toys when you want him to.

Signs of dominance are:
1. Makes eye contact.
2. Stands with ears up, tail up and the hair raised on his neck.
3. Shows dominance over another dog by standing at right angles over it.

Dominant dogs tend to behave in characteristic ways such as:
1. The dog may be unwilling to move from his place (i.e., reluctant to give up the sofa if the owner wants to sit there).
2. He may not part with toys or objects in his mouth and may show possessiveness with his food bowl.
3. He may not respond quickly to commands.
4. He may be disagreeable for grooming and dislikes to be petted.

Dogs are popular because of their sociable nature. Those that have contact with humans during the first 12 weeks of life regard them as a member of their own species—their pack. All dogs have the potential for both dominant and submissive behavior. Only through experience and training do they learn to whom it is appropriate to show which behavior. Not all dogs are concerned with dominance but owners need to be aware of that potential. It is wise for the owner to establish his dominance early on.

Don't let that innocent face fool you! Like all puppies, three-month-old Fanfair Tailwind is ready, willing, and able to get into plenty of mischief.

A human can express dominance or submission toward a dog in the following ways:

1. Meeting the dog's gaze signals dominance. Averting the gaze signals submission. If the dog growls or threatens, averting the gaze is the first avoiding action to take—it may prevent attack. It is important to establish eye contact in the puppy. The older dog that has not been exposed to eye contact may see it as a threat and will not be willing to submit.

2. Being taller than the dog signals dominance; being lower signals submission. This is why, when attempting to make friends with a strange dog or catch the runaway, one should kneel down to his level. Some owners see their

dogs become dominant when allowed on the furniture or on the bed. Then he is at the owner's level.

3. An owner can gain dominance by ignoring all the dog's social initiatives. The owner pays attention to the dog only when he obeys a command.

No dog should be allowed to achieve dominant status over any adult or child. Ways of preventing are as follows:

1. Handle the puppy gently, especially during the three-to four-month period.

Your Lhasa puppy may display fear at certain times. Respect his feelings and give him time to become used to the situation.

2. Let the children and adults handfeed him and teach him to take food without lunging or grabbing.

3. Do not allow him to chase children or joggers.

4. Do not allow him to jump on

people or mount their legs. Even females may be inclined to mount. It is not only a male habit.

5. Do not allow him to growl for any reason.

6. Don't participate in wrestling or tug-of-war games.

7. Don't physically punish puppies for aggressive behavior. Restrain him from repeating the infraction and teach an alternative behavior. Dogs should earn everything they receive from their owners. This would include sitting to receive petting or treats, sitting before going out the door and sitting to receive the collar and leash. These types of exercises reinforce the owner's dominance.

Young children should never be left alone with a dog. It is important that children learn some basic obedience commands so they have some control over the dog. They will gain the respect of their dog.

FEAR

One of the most common problems dogs experience is being fearful. Some dogs are more afraid than others. On the lesser side, which is sometimes humorous to watch, dogs can be afraid of a strange object. They act silly when something is out of place in the house. We call his problem perceptive intelligence. He realizes the abnormal within his known environment. He does not react the same way in strange environments since he does not know what is normal.

On the more serious side is a fear of people. This can result in backing off, seeking his own space and saying "leave me alone" or it can result in an aggressive behavior that may lead to challenging the person. Respect that the dog wants to be left alone and give him time to come forward. If you approach the cornered dog, he may resort to snapping. If you leave him alone, he may decide to come forward, which should be rewarded with a treat.

Some dogs may initially be too fearful to take treats. In these cases it is helpful to make sure the dog hasn't eaten for about 24 hours. Being a little hungry encourages him to accept the treats, especially if they are of the "gourmet" variety.

Dogs can be afraid of numerous things, including loud noises and thunderstorms. Invariably the owner

Although a Christmas puppy may sound like a wonderful idea, the holidays are the worst time of year to bring a new dog home.

Responsible breeding and the proper upbringing can help to ensure your puppy has a good temperament.

rewards (by comforting) the dog when it shows signs of fearfulness. When your dog is frightened, direct his attention to something else and act happy. Don't dwell on his fright.

AGGRESSION

Some different types of aggression are: predatory, defensive, dominance, possessive, protective, fear induced, noise provoked, "rage" syndrome (unprovoked aggression), maternal and aggression directed toward other dogs. Aggression is the most common behavioral problem encountered. Protective breeds are expected to be more aggressive than others but with the proper upbringing they can make very dependable companions. You need to be able to read your dog.

Many factors contribute to aggression including genetics and environment. An improper environment, which may include the living conditions, lack of social life, excessive punishment, being attacked or frightened by an aggressive dog, etc., can all influence a dog's behavior. Even spoiling him and giving too much praise may be detrimental. Isolation and the lack of human contact or exposure to frequent teasing by children or adults also can ruin a good dog.

Lack of direction, fear, or confusion lead to aggression in those dogs that are so inclined. Any obedience exercise, even the sit and down, can direct the dog and overcome fear and/or confusion. Every dog should learn these commands as a youngster, and there should be periodic reinforcement.

When a dog is showing signs of aggression, you should speak calmly (no screaming or hysterics) and firmly give a command that he understands, such as the sit. As soon as your dog obeys, you have assumed your dominant position. Aggression presents a problem because there may be danger to others. Sometimes it is an emotional issue. Owners may consciously or unconsciously encourage their dog's aggression. Other owners show responsibility by accepting the problem and taking measures to keep it under control. The owner is responsible for his dog's actions, and it is not wise to take a chance on someone being bitten, especially a child. Euthanasia is the solution for some owners and in severe cases this may be the best choice. However, few dogs are that dangerous and very few are that much of a threat to their owners. If caution is exercised and professional help is gained early on, most cases can be controlled.

Some authorities recommend feeding a lower protein (less than 20 percent) diet. They believe this can aid in reducing aggression. If the dog loses weight, then vegetable oil can be added. Veterinarians and behaviorists are having some success with pharmacology. In many cases treatment is possible and can improve the situation.

Make sure your Lhasa has plenty of safe toys to keep him occupied and his teeth healthy.

If you have done everything according to "the book" regarding training and socializing and are still having a behavior problem, don't procrastinate. It is important that the problem gets attention before it is out of hand. It is estimated that 20 percent of a veterinarian's time may be devoted to dealing with problems before they become so

Giving your Lhasa plenty of exercise, attention, and toys can prevent certain problem behavior.

intolerable that the dog is separated from its home and owner. If your veterinarian isn't able to help, he should refer you to a behaviorist.

PROBLEMS

Barking

This is a habit that shouldn't be encouraged. Some owners desire their dog to bark so as to be a watchdog. Most dogs will bark when a stranger comes to the door.

The new puppy frequently barks or whines in the crate in his strange environment and the owner reinforces the puppy's bad behavior by going to him during the night. This is a no-no. Smack the top of the crate and say "quiet" in a loud, firm voice. The puppies don't like to hear the loud noise of the crate being banged. If the barking is sleep-interrupting, then the owner should take crate and pup to the bedroom for a few days until the puppy becomes adjusted to his new environment. Otherwise ignore the barking during the night.

Barking can be an inherited problem or a bad habit learned through the environment. It takes dedication to stop the barking. Attention should be paid to the cause of the barking. Does the dog seek attention, does he need to go out, is it feeding time, is it occurring when he is left alone, is it a protective bark, etc.? Overzealous barking is an inherited tendency. When barking presents a problem for you, try to stop it as soon as it begins.

There are electronic collars available that are supposed to curb barking. There are some disadvantages to to the collar. If the dog is barking out of excitement, punishment is not the appropriate treatment. Presumably there is the chance the collar could be activated by other stimuli and thereby punish the dog when it is not barking. Should you decide to use one, then you should seek help from a person with experience with that type of collar. Nevertheless the root of the problem needs to be investigated and corrected.

It has been found that spending time with pets can reduce stress and improve your quality of life.

In extreme circumstances (usually when there is a problem with the neighbors), some people have resorted to having their dogs debarked. I caution you that the dog continues to bark but usually only a squeaking sound is heard. Frequently the vocal cords grow back. Probably the biggest concern is that the dog can be left with scar tissue which can narrow the opening to the trachea.

Jumping Up

A dog that jumps up is a happy dog. Nevertheless few guests appreciate dogs jumping on them. Clothes get footprinted and/or snagged.

Some trainers believe in allowing the puppy to jump up during his first few weeks. If you correct him too soon and at the wrong age you may intimidate him. Consequently he could be timid around humans later in his life. However, there will come a time, probably around four months of age, that he needs to know when it is okay to jump and when he is to show off good manners by sitting instead.

Some authorities never allow jumping. If you are irritated by your dog jumping up on you, then you should discourage it from the beginning. A larger breed of dog can cause harm to a senior citizen. Some are quite fragile. It may not take much to cause a topple that could break a hip.

How do you correct the problem? All family members need to participate in teaching the puppy to sit as soon as he starts to jump up. The sit must be practiced every time he starts to jump up. Don't forget to praise him for his good behavior. If an

older dog has acquired the habit, grasp his paws and squeeze tightly. Give a firm "No." He'll soon catch on. Remember the entire family must take part. Each time you allow him to jump up you go back a step in training.

Biting

All puppies bite and try to chew on your fingers, toes, arms, etc. This is the time to teach them to be gentle and not bite hard. Put your fingers in your puppy's mouth and if he bites too hard then say "easy" and let him know he's hurting you. Squeal and act like you have been seriously hurt. If the puppy plays too rough and doesn't respond to your corrections, then he needs "Time Out" in his crate. You should be particularly careful with young children and puppies who still have their deciduous (baby) teeth. Those teeth are like needles and can leave little scars on youngsters.

Biting in the more mature dog is something that should be prevented at all costs. Should it occur quickly let him know in no uncertain terms that biting will not be tolerated. When biting is directed toward another dog (dog fight), don't get in the middle of it. Some authorities recommend breaking up a fight by elevating the hind legs. This would only be possible if there was a person for each dog. Obviously it would be hard to fight with the hind legs off the ground. A dog bite is serious and should be given attention. Wash the bite with soap and water and contact your doctor. It is important to know the status of the offender's rabies vaccination.

Your dog must know who is boss. When biting occurs, you should seek professional help at once. On the other hand you must not let your dog intimidate you and be so afraid of a bite that you can't discipline him. Professional help through your veterinarian, dog trainer, breeder, and/or behaviorist can give you guidance.

Digging

Bored dogs release their frustrations through mischievous behavior such as digging. Dogs shouldn't be left unattended outside, even if they are in a fenced-in yard. Usually the dog is sent to "jail" (the backyard) because the owner can't tolerate him in the house. The culprit feels socially deprived and needs to be included in the owner's life. The owner has neglected the dog's training. The dog has not developed into the companion we desire. If you are one of these owners, then perhaps it is possible for you to change. Give him another chance. Some owners object to their dog's unkempt coat and doggy odor. See that he is groomed on a regular schedule and look into some training classes.

Submissive Urination

This is not a housebreaking problem. It can occur in all breeds and may be more prevalent in some breeds. Usually it occurs in puppies but occasionally it occurs in older dogs and may be in response to physical praise. Try verbal praise or ignoring your dog until after he has had a chance to relieve himself. Scolding will only make the problem worse. Many dogs outgrow this problem.

Coprophagia

Also know as stool eating, sometimes occurs without a cause. It may begin with boredom and then becomes a habit that is hard to break. Your best remedy is to keep the puppy on a leash and keep the yard picked up. Then he

Provide your pup with plenty of toys and activities to keep boredom at bay.

won't have an opportunity to get in trouble. Your veterinarian can dispense a medication that is put on the dog's food that makes the stool taste bitter. Of course this will do little good if your dog cleans up after other dogs.

The Runaway

There is little excuse for a dog to run away since dogs should never be off leash except when supervised in the fenced-in yard.

Many prospective owners that want to purchase a female since a male is inclined to roam. It is true that an intact male is inclined to roam, which is one of the reasons a male should be neutered. However, females will roam also, especially if they are in heat. Regardless, these dogs should never be given this opportunity. A few years ago one of our clients elected euthanasia for her elderly dog that radiographically appeared to have an intestinal blockage. The veterinarian suggested it might be a corncob. She assured him that was not possible since they hadn't had any. Apparently he roamed and raided the neighbor's garbage and you guessed it—he had a corncob blocking his intestines. Another dog raided the neighbor's garbage and died from toxins from the garbage.

To give the benefit of the doubt, perhaps your dog escapes or perhaps you are playing with your dog in the yard and he refuses to come when called. You now have a runaway. Help! The first thing to remember is when you finally do catch your naughty dog, you must not discipline him. The reasoning behind this is that it is quite possible there could be a repeat performance, and it would be nice if the next time he would respond to your sweet command.

Always kneel down when trying to catch the runaway. Dogs are afraid of people standing over them. Also it would be helpful to have a treat or a favorite toy to help entice him to your side. After that initial runaway experience, start practicing the recall with your dog. You can let him drag a long line (clothesline) and randomly call him and then reel him in. Let him touch you first. Reaching for the dog can frighten him. Each time he comes you reward him with a treat and eventually he should get the idea that this is a nice experience. The long line prevents him from really getting out of hand. At least with the long line you can step on it and stop him.

SUGGESTED READING

RE-331
Guide to Owning a
Lhasa Apso
64 pages, 50 full-color
photos.

TS-214
Owner's Guide to Dog
Health
224 pages, over 190
full-color photos.

TS-257
Choosing a Dog for Life
384 pages, over 800
full-color photos.

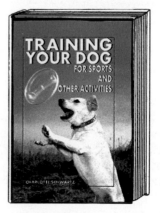

TS-258
Training Your Dog for
Sports and Other Activities
160 pages, over 200
full-color photos.

INDEX

Independence
Township
Library

Clarkston, Michigan

Independence
Township
Library

Clarkston, Michigan

WITHDRAWN

INDEPENDENCE TOWNSHIP LIBRARY
6495 CLARKSTON ROAD
CLARKSTON, MI 48346-1501